Morteza Kohansal
Maryam Salehilalehmarzi

Good To Great: Leaders eat last

Morteza Kohansal
Maryam Salehilalehmarzi

Good To Great: Leaders eat last

Management

LAP LAMBERT Academic Publishing

Imprint

Any brand names and product names mentioned in this book are subject to trademark, brand or patent protection and are trademarks or registered trademarks of their respective holders. The use of brand names, product names, common names, trade names, product descriptions etc. even without a particular marking in this work is in no way to be construed to mean that such names may be regarded as unrestricted in respect of trademark and brand protection legislation and could thus be used by anyone.

Cover image: www.ingimage.com

Publisher:
LAP LAMBERT Academic Publishing
is a trademark of
International Book Market Service Ltd., member of OmniScriptum Publishing Group
17 Meldrum Street, Beau Bassin 71504, Mauritius

Printed at: see last page
ISBN: 978-620-0-50244-5

Good To Great:
Leaders eat last

Corresponding Authors:

Prof. Dr. Morteza Kohansal; Robert Gordon University, Head of Iranian Elite Academy.
Maryam Salehilalehmarzi.

Email : Morteza.Kohansal@outlook.com

2020

CONTENTS OF BOOK

Are you a growth leader? The seven beliefs and behaviors that growth leaders share

A new survey highlights what separates growth leaders from the pack.

What makes someone a growth leader? In conversations we've had with business leaders, the answer tends to boil down to a variation of "I know it when I see it." But it turns out that there is a specific set of attributes that growth leaders share.

After carrying out a survey of 165 C-suite executives and senior vice presidents with growth responsibilities and conducting in-depth interviews with 20 executives, we found that growth leaders   have seven specific beliefs and behaviors.

Furthermore, our research shows that executives who adopt more than 70 percent of these mind-sets manage to grow their top line twice as fast as their peers. We've boiled down these beliefs and behaviors to seven statements that reflect the convictions of today's growth leaders.

1. I am all in.

Always put growth first. Growth leaders put growth at the top of every agenda, from board meetings to performance reviews. As the president of a global consumer goods company put it, "Growth is priority number one, two, and three." This disciplined focus on growth is reflected

4

in a profound belief that "growth is everywhere" and opportunities to outgrow peers can be found in every industry.

That mind-set is supported by our research. From other McKinsey analysis, our findings show that there is a growth-capability gap of 20 to 46 percentage points between top and bottom performers. This indicates that growth is possible in any industry when growth leaders back up their faith with committed action.

Growth leaders also demonstrate this kind of commitment by constantly scouring for funds to invest in growth. They have a clear vision of where every incremental dollar they find should be invested, and they actively manage that allocation by helping those affected (shareholders, owners) understand why.

Keep raising the bar. No matter how ambitious growth targets are, the legacy business will revert to business as usual unless constantly challenged to be more aspirational. Growth leaders do this by setting targets that seem almost impossible to reach, forcing teams to strive for greater impact. The CMO at one tech company told us that the CEO set growth targets at three times the market rate, adding, "We exceeded two-and-a-half times market growth. We were rewarded for pushing hard and not hurt if we failed."

> Growth leaders are 50% more likely to treat growth as the first or second item on the agenda when speaking to the board

Unite the business around growth. Growth leaders make growth the central focus of everyone in the business by creating a common belief and language. For example, they cocreate growth goals and metrics with their leadership teams and then help translate them into metrics for every individual at every level. Establishing this kind of shared and cocreated language binds employees together to think about how they can contribute to top-line growth. One technology-company leader created a single set of growth targets that tied directly to the incentives of 250 managers across the business: "Whether you're in legal, marketing, sales, or service, you're bound by the same aspirations."

2. I am willing to fail.

Make plenty of bets. Growth leaders make more growth bets than their peers. They create a portfolio of initiatives, protecting the necessary resources and funding. In fact, growth leaders in Europe are 70 percent more likely to make multiple growth bets rather than just a couple. By managing a scaled portfolio of growth bets, they improve their probabilities of success while diversifying risk. A former tech-company board member explained, "Winning big has such huge rewards that it's more important than how often you lose."

> Growth leaders are 70% more likely to make multiple long-term growth bets rather than just a few (in the European Union)

Back the risk takers. Effective leaders have always been good at delegating, but growth leaders go a step further by instilling a culture that empowers people to make decisions. Some 40 percent of growth leaders in North America, for example, are more likely to be comfortable with middle managers and frontline employees making important decisions.

> Growth leaders are 70% more likely to protect or set aside money in the budget to fund growth initiatives, teams, and capabilities (in North America)

Growth leaders set clear and ambitious goals (#1) and communicate progress effectively to the business (#6), but then they step out of the way so that people in the business can iterate on solutions to deliver on the growth aspirations. That starts by encouraging risk taking even at the smallest level and celebrating rather than punishing people for trying. As a former CMO of a technology company put it, "If you want people to lead your business into growth, things will go wrong. Having support helps people become risk takers." EU growth leaders are 40 percent more likely to have explicit incentives to reward risk taking in their teams.

3. I know my customer as a person, not as a data point.

> Growth leaders are 70% more likely to build an understanding of customers' needs through formal and informal methods (ethnography, surveys, in-store visits, etc)

Take the customer's side. Most business leaders believe they put the customer first. But the truth is that the pressures of leading a large business—shareholder relations, risk management, and so on—mean that the customer too often becomes an afterthought. Growth leaders are resolute, however, in putting the customer at the center of all their decisions. An executive at a global apparel brand admitted, "Whenever I'm in meetings and being presented with options to decide on, my first question is, 'What's in it for the customer?'"

> Growth leaders are 50% more likely to build an organization that puts the customer first (in North America)

Make it personal. Many of the best companies have strong customer-insights organizations. Customer insights and analytics are crucial to supporting growth. But growth leaders go the extra mile by embracing design thinking and taking the time to build empathy with the customer. As the executive at a manufacturing company, who spent a whole day shadowing one customer, put it: "I followed this customer from 6:30 in the morning until he went home at the end of the day. That gave me so much insight into what he needed, what his fears were, and what we could do as a company."

4. I favor action over perfection.

Put yourself on the line. Growth decisions can make or break a career. Growth leaders aren't afraid to take that risk. That can mean trading short-term gains for long-term benefit or making large resource-reallocation decisions. But they understand that that's what's needed for growth, and they role-model the behavior they want others to adopt.

When the managing director of a transport company lowered prices to increase its number of passengers by 20 percent in a declining market, this director accepted the need for bold moves: "Growth is worth the risk." Whenever a new-customer offer was planned, the pricing team would work out how much value was at risk and put it in a document. The director would then sign it, making a public declaration to take on this risk personally.

Act on "good enough" insights. Good data are crucial for good decisions, but growth leaders value speed over perfect insights. They don't wait for perfect data. Instead, they use the data they have to make a thoughtful decision, pursue it vigorously, and then reevaluate based on results. As one growth leader from a tech company explained, "Always look for opportunities around you, and be willing to jump."

> Growth leaders are 70% more likely to prioritize speed over perfection (in North America)

Face the facts. When the facts are clear that a business or product is underperforming, growth leaders are decisive in killing them off. Continually allocating resources to proven growth options or new initiatives that promise a better return on investment is a crucial leadership discipline, even if it means saying goodbye to beloved brands or products. The leader at one fast-moving consumer-goods (FMCG) company instituted a process that labeled any service or product that wasn't yielding growth a "zombie." Leadership sent business units a quarterly hit list that helped the company eliminate 700 zombies within a year.

5. I fight for growth.

Avoid short-termism. Leaders face huge pressures to deliver results in the short term. While growth leaders understand that reality, they don't sacrifice long-term growth. To help guard against those pressures, they make deliberate resource-allocation decisions that position the business for future growth. As the CMO of a telecom company put it, "I assign 50 percent of resources to the first year, 30 percent to the second year, and 20 percent to year three. That means you don't keep falling off a cliff at the end of every year, and you build sustainable growth."

Growth leaders are also vigilant in keeping the organization from clawing back those resources, as so often happens. Among leaders in North America, 70 percent are more likely than their peers to protect or set aside money in the budget to fund growth initiatives, teams, and capabilities.

Break down internal barriers. Growth is a team sport, but functional leaders often jealously guard their turf, which undermines many promising initiatives. Growth leaders actively seek out the conflicts and eliminate them. They break down silos, diffuse turf battles, and provide support for strained resources to clear the path for their teams to deliver.

The leader at a global beverages company, for example, created a central growth office to merge marketing, customer insights, and commercial groups into one unit with a clear mandate—and shared accountability—for growth. This move helped eliminate the functional silos that were impeding progress.

> Growth leaders are 60% more likely to have a clear multiyear mandate to pursue growth initiatives, coupled with the autonomy to do so without having to show short-term results

6. I have a growth story I tell all the time.

Infuse the business with purpose. Growth leaders know that purpose is power and that communication is about more than the what of growth; it's the why. Articulating a purpose that goes beyond brands, categories, and businesses is an effective way that growth leaders rally the whole organization. Growth leaders in the European Union are, for example, 70 percent more likely to ensure that every employee understands the growth strategy and what it means for them. Says the CMO of a major consumer company: "Everybody needs purpose. Employees thrive on it, society expects it, and it delivers growth."

> Growth leaders are 80% more likely to communicate growth successes often (in the European Union)

Communicate, communicate, communicate. While business leaders understand the need to communicate, they tend to underestimate its importance. Not so, growth leaders. They communicate clearly, creatively, and consistently. Growth leaders in the European Union, for example, are 80 percent more likely than their peers to communicate growth successes often.

> Growth leaders are 70% more likely to ensure that every employee understands the growth strategy and what it means for them (in the European Union)

They also go beyond the usual channels (progress updates, newsletters, town halls, and the like) and develop a comprehensive communications plan targeting all stakeholders. They often, for example, tell their story to the outside world in order to motivate employees, shape investor perceptions, and convey their aspirations to customers. The managing director of one consumer-facing company told us, "Use the media to communicate wins, results, and innovation. Make it real for all your stakeholders as often as possible."

7. I give control to others.

Build up people's growth muscles. Growth leaders invest more time in formal and informal training for growth, covering not just functional and leadership capabilities but also mind-sets. At one global beverages company, training for marketing and sales associates includes elements on exponential thinking (working toward tenfold improvements rather than 10 percent) and using network effects to boost growth (engaging stakeholders and ecosystems to boost a product launch or a marketing campaign).

Give power to the front line. Encouraging people to make decisions and take risks without providing them with a structure for doing so is only half the battle. Growth leaders are explicit in giving people decision rights. The owner of a European digital company ensures that key decisions are made not by senior management but by the business-unit leaders who know the customers and products best. But those leaders have to work together across functions. As the chief growth officer of a leading consumer-packaged-goods company put it: "Product, engineering, and sales take decisions jointly, so you don't have fingers pointing at each other."

Go outside to get what's needed. Growth leaders aren't afraid to close gaps in their own business models or capabilities through partnerships or joint ventures with other businesses. A travel company wanted to expand its low-cost bus business but realized it was too small to compete at scale with larger companies. To acquire sufficient scale at speed, it partnered with a ride-sharing platform to offer a door-to-door long-distance service that combined rail, bus, and car transport in one convenient package.

> Growth leaders are 40% more likely to have explicit incentives to reward risk taking in their teams (in the European Union)

10

Growth is a journey that requires the entire business to constantly adjust, optimize, and execute, but it starts at the top. Only when the CEO, C-suite, and business-unit leaders have the right mind-set can leaders hope to drive growth across the business.

1. For the purposes of our research, we defined growth leaders as executives of companies that achieved a compound annual growth rate more than 4 percent higher than their peers, coupled with higher profit margins. Respondents came from both North America and the European Union, and occasionally there were regional variations in their methodology.

Marketing's moment is now: The C-suite partnership to deliver on growth

Is your marketing executive a Unifier, Loner, or Friend? The CMO's rapport with the C-suite is crucial in establishing marketing's role as a growth driver.

Marketing's big opportunity is here. CEOs are turning to marketing to drive their company's growth agenda, and they're giving CMOs the runway and support to do so.

In a new McKinsey study, 83 percent of global CEOs say that marketing can be a major driver of growth. For a function that has all too often been thought of as the "brand" or "advertising" arm of the business, this is a notable development. But the news isn't all rosy. Some 23 percent of CEOs do not feel that marketing is *delivering* on that agenda, and the view elsewhere in the C-suite is even more mixed. One group of CMOs, however, has figured out how to deliver on the growth promise (Exhibit 1).

Exhibit 1

CEOs see marketing as owning the growth agenda.

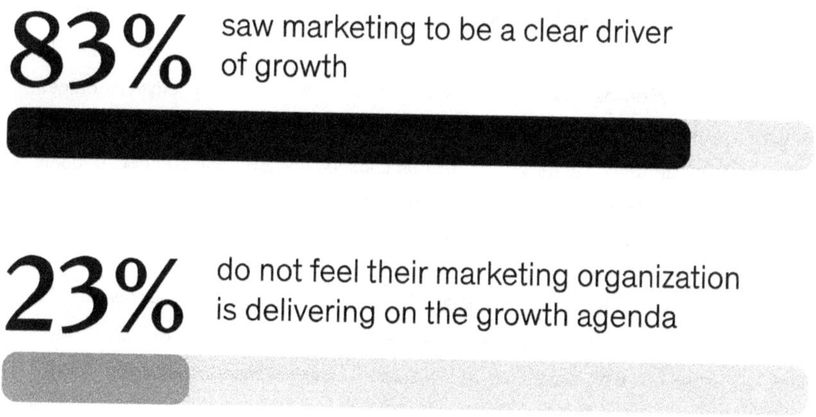

83% saw marketing to be a clear driver of growth

23% do not feel their marketing organization is delivering on the growth agenda

C-suite view of marketing

In recent years, a sea change has occurred at leading companies. Executives at these organizations no longer view marketing as bound by functions that sit in the marketing department. Instead, they think in terms of what we call "marketing with a capital M." In this model, diverse areas of the organization—from sales and product innovation to finance, technology, and HR—participate in marketing's success and see themselves as partners in its mission. As head of marketing, the CMO has a crucial role to play in driving organizations toward this vision, and the stakes are high. Our analysis reveals that a marketing organization's ability to drive growth depends heavily on the strength of the partnerships the CMO can forge across the organization. We call these CMOs Unifiers.

To build deep, productive relationships, CMOs have to win over some skeptics in the C-suite. Only half the CFOs we surveyed, for example, said marketing delivers on the promise of driving growth, and 40 percent don't think marketing investments should be protected during a downturn. There is even less symbiosis between marketing and the chief human resources officer (CHRO)—a big Achilles heel, given the need to attract the world-class talent that will allow marketing organizations to thrive. Further complicating matters, just 3 percent of board members have a marketing background. "Everyone [on the board] has an opinion about marketing, but there is very little expertise," noted one former apparel CEO.

Overcoming these hurdles isn't just essential for the CMO; it's crucial for the business's growth. Our analysis shows that high-growth companies are seven times more likely to have a **Unifier** CMO—someone who fosters robust, collaborative partnerships across the C-suite—as the more isolated archetype we call **Loner**. Most marketers are somewhere in between, an archetype we call **Friend** (Exhibit 2).

Exhibit 2

Today's CMOs break into three different archetypes.

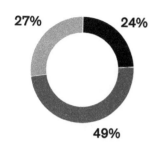

27%   24%

49%

● **Unifier**
Strong partnership with key players in C-suite to drive growth

◍ **Loner**
Limited relationship with C-suite focused primarily on marketing communications

● **Friend**
Good relationship with 1-2 of C-suite, especially CEO, with limited responsibility for growth and customer experience

Meet the three CMO archetypes

If Julius Caesar were a modern executive, he might say that, like Gaul, all CMOs are divided into three parts, each with distinctive habits and traits: the Unifier, the Friend, and the Loner. However, only one—the Unifier—is the key to future victory.

Unifiers

These CMOs are masters at fostering cross-functional collaboration. They ensure that marketing has a clearly defined role in the eyes of C-suite peers; they adopt the language and mindset of other C-suite executives; and they articulate how marketing can help meet the C-suite's needs. They also establish mutual accountability and a shared vision with other executives. Sought after by peers for advice, they have a seat at the table when critical decisions are made, have broad profit-and-loss (P&L) responsibility, and are often involved in defining the company's strategy. As a result, their budgets are more likely to be protected during a downturn, and they enjoy a 48 percent longer tenure. Unifiers may be born or made. Aside from inherent leadership abilities, the organizational and cultural conditions for creating Unifiers can be established by the CEO.

Loners

These CMOs may be great marketers, but they don't have the full support of, or deep relationships with, their C-suite peers. Loners tend to focus on near-term activities like ad campaigns and social media. They are seen by CEOs as executors of brand stewardship, advertising, and PR, not as equal partners. They are more likely to implement strategy than develop it and often report that their CEO doesn't understand or trust marketing. "If a campaign goes well, it's because the sales team did well. If it goes bad, it's marketing's fault," one former entertainment president told us, summing up the challenges of working with a Loner CMO.

Friends

This most prevalent type of CMO lies somewhere between Unifier and Loner. The Friend has one or two allies in the C-suite, often the CEO, but hasn't been able to spread marketing's agenda fully across the organization. Responsible for top-line growth through marketing channels, Friend CMOs typically don't have broad P&L responsibility or even much influence across the entirety of customer experience, such as product development and customer service. They are also not as adept at speaking the language of the C-suite, and chief technical officers (CTOs) tend to see them as "customers" of technology rather than as partners in driving innovation and developing new capabilities.

What Unifiers do well

Unifier CMOs excel in four areas in which they work directly with relevant members of the C-suite to drive the business's growth agenda.

Exhibit 3

Key Unifier CMO relationship-building traits.

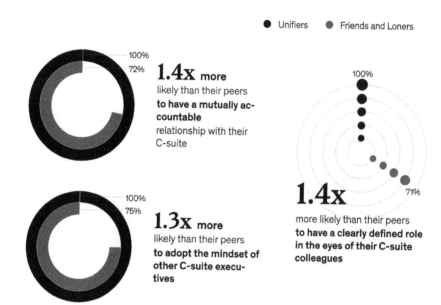

● Unifiers   ● Friends and Loners

100%
72%

1.4x more
likely than their peers
**to have a mutually ac-
countable**
relationship with their
C-suite

100%
75%

1.3x more
likely than their peers
**to adopt the mindset of
other C-suite execu-
tives**

100%

71%

1.4x
more likely than their peers
**to have a clearly defined role
in the eyes of their C-suite
colleagues**

Fully leveraging CEO support to help drive growth

Unifier CMOs know the CEO is firmly in their corner, and they use this support to further marketing's growth agenda. They start by making sure the CEO understands how exactly marketing is driving growth, owning the customer, and serving the company's broader goals and objectives. Unifiers weave many sources of insight and a deep understanding of the customer into a holistic picture of opportunity that the CMO and CEO jointly translate into short- and long-term initiatives.

These CMOs are viewed as peers and called upon by CEOs for insight and early detection of changes in customer habits that will impact the business. Unifiers elevate marketing's role by developing a deep understanding of end-to-end customer journeys. Thanks to such mutual accountability and shared mind-sets, they report meaningfully more support and buy-in for marketing's agenda from CEOs than Loners (Exhibit 4).

Exhibit 4

Unifiers report meaningfully more support and buy-in for marketing's agenda from CEOs than Loners.

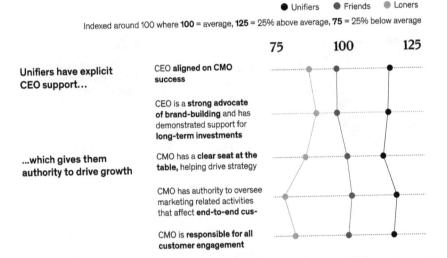

● Unifiers   ● Friends   ● Loners

Indexed around 100 where **100** = average, **125** = 25% above average, **75** = 25% below average

	75	100	125

Unifiers have explicit CEO support...

CEO **aligned on CMO success**

CEO is a **strong advocate of brand-building** and has demonstrated support for **long-term investments**

...which gives them authority to drive growth

CMO has a **clear seat at the table,** helping drive strategy

CMO has authority to oversee marketing related activities that affect **end-to-end cus-**

CMO is **responsible for all customer engagement**

"Marketing as a support function is antiquated," said the CEO of an apparel company with a Unifier CMO. These leaders are also given greater authority to oversee marketing-related activities that may not reside in marketing but affect the end-to-end customer journey, such as product and customer service. They are twice as likely as Loner CMOs to be responsible for all customer engagement and value creation, and roughly three times as likely to have oversight over the end-to-end customer journey.

There is at least one area where Unifier CMOs have room to grow, however. Many CEOs want marketers to think big and take risks that could pay off—something CMOs don't always realize. The former CEO of a leading retailer told us that he was a huge believer in the value of marketing, more so than anyone else in the C-suite. Yet his CMO still sometimes asked for permission instead of assuming co-ownership of the challenge.

Adopting the mind-set of a CFO to establish marketing as a driver of value

If the CEO is a CMO's closest natural ally, the CFO is one of her toughest critics. "Under pressure, marketing gets cut first because it is the hardest to justify," said one former consumer-goods CFO we interviewed. Forty-five percent of CFOs we surveyed said the reason marketing proposals have been declined or not fully funded in the past is because they didn't demonstrate a clear line to value.

To overcome this, Unifier CMOs demonstrate that marketing is accountable and does in fact drive predictable and significant value. The best marketers use advanced analytics to help quantify the impact that marketing spend has on short- and long-term value. They build business cases with metrics that reflect meaningful financial value (ROI, customer lifetime value, revenue run rate) rather than more prevalent but less valid—in the CFO's eyes, anyway —indicators, such as brand equity, gross rating points (GRPs), or engagement. "Embrace metrics that matter," said one telecommunications CFO. "Come to me and tell me what the right ones are."

Unifier CMOs don't just adopt financial lingo for their interactions with the CFO; they incorporate quantitative rigor as well as profit-and-loss accountability into every decision they make. They jointly own the vision, coming to agreements about what each other's needs are and which initiatives and key performance indicators (KPIs) are important, with the CMO reporting back regularly with progress updates. Artful CMOs are able to do this while still supporting a culture of innovation and experimentation. One tech CMO, for instance, worked with his CFO to cocreate a "fighting fund" that looked for marketing efficiencies and funneled a portion of the savings into a reinvestment fund that marketers could access for projects with a clear ROI. The availability of new funding incentivized marketers to think of innovative approaches.

CFOs who appreciate marketing's value are also far more likely to preserve its budget in difficult times. At one apparel company, where the CMO has a collaborative relationship with the CFO, it's the CFO who asserts, "We are not going to touch the marketing budget."

Partnering with the CTO to unlock the power of data

Companies with Unifier CMOs understand that marketing and technology are inextricable partners in developing capabilities for unlocking value in new ways. Marketing simply can't take advantage of the vast volume of data companies possess without close collaboration with the CTO.

As partners, they develop a shared vision of how data from separate, disconnected systems can be integrated and then used to understand customers at granular levels, personalize interactions, and predict customer behavior. At a leading retailer, the CTO joined the CMO in taking accountability for the digital transformation of marketing, repeatedly presenting their vision and budget requirements to the operating committee and board until they got full buy-in.

CTOs who feel responsible for the outcomes of marketing initiatives are more likely to devote dedicated resources to them. Unifier CMOs are about three times as likely as Loners to have their own dedicated data-analytics teams, for example, which help improve the quality and speed of marketing decisions. At one direct-to-consumer entertainment company, the CMO used to "beg" for support from IT. That changed after the company did a multiyear migration to cloud platforms and adopted an agile model in which marketing and tech teams work side by side in pods to accomplish shared goals. These shifts helped the company drive an 11 percent increase in top-line revenue (Exhibit 5).

Exhibit 5

Unifiers have the analytics resources they need.

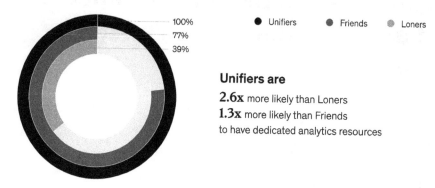

100%
77%
39%

● Unifiers   ● Friends   ● Loners

Unifiers are

2.6x more likely than Loners
1.3x more likely than Friends
to have dedicated analytics resources

Empowering the CHRO to win the war for talent

All CMOs, regardless of their leadership archetype, understand that driving performance requires access to world-class marketing talent, never an easy thing to come by. Although companies with Unifiers are roughly three times more likely than those with Loners to attract and develop talent that balances analytics and creativity, they still report difficulty in meeting their talent needs (Exhibit 6).

Exhibit 6

Unifiers have the right balance of analytics and creative talent.

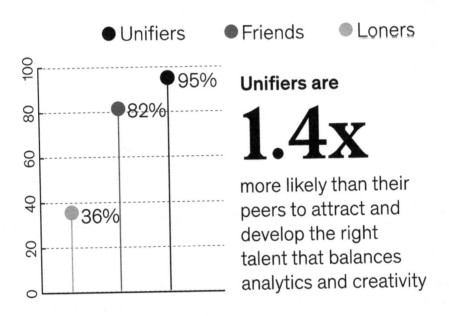

● Unifiers   ● Friends   ● Loners

Unifiers are

1.4x

more likely than their peers to attract and develop the right talent that balances analytics and creativity

95%

82%

36%

Overall there is a massive talent gap: a whopping 82 percent of Fortune 500 executives don't believe they recruit highly talented people.   Relying on legacy recruiting and training programs won't do. The CMO can play a critical and influential role here by engaging with the CHRO, educating her about marketing's diverse talent requirements and the need to evolve the organization's culture for the next generation. Together, the CMO and CHRO can develop new job classifications and devise innovative ways of building talent, from going all out to hire anchor talent and building new careers paths to creating talent war rooms that can recruit more quickly. Setting up internal academies to reskill and upskill existing marketers and non-marketers can help people keep pace with changes in the marketplace.

Arguably, there has never been a better time to be a CMO. CEOs are giving CMOs permission to step up and think boldly about how marketing can drive growth. But CMOs also need to give themselves permission to assume the growth mantle. Being a modern, highly effective CMO means taking on ambitious ideas, unifying the C-suite, and transforming other leaders into champions of the marketing agenda.

But CMOs can't do it alone. CEOs will need to look at their role in supporting the CMO and whether the company's operating model supports cross-functional collaboration. The rest of the C-suite will need to fully embrace the potential of marketing and see a CMO partnership as an opportunity to help drive growth and deliver real value for the organization. Ultimately, the C-suite needs to ask itself: Is the CMO empowered to function as a Unifier or is she destined to be a Loner or Friend?

Growing faster than the market: Three questions the C-suite should ask

Leaders who are most successful at driving growth in their organizations are deliberate, persistent, and disciplined in the way they go about it.

Growing a business is a matter of do or die. Consider the fate of the 100 largest companies on the New York Stock Exchange of 30 years ago. Among those that enjoyed strong shareholder returns but didn't post top-line growth, almost 50 percent had been acquired or delisted 20 years later. Companies with high organic growth also return a better stock price.

But growth is getting tougher in the face of new market dynamics: rising consumer expectations, increasing competition, and digital disruption. That has turned growth into more of a contact sport, rewarding businesses that can spot opportunities at hypergranular levels and then capture them quickly.

Most business leaders understand the need to change, but making it happen is easier said than done. In our experience, those leaders who are most successful at driving growth in their organizations are deliberate and disciplined in the way they do it. To help instill that approach, top growth leaders are methodical in asking and answering three crucial questions:

1. Where is my growth going to come from?

2. How do I grow now and tomorrow?

3. How do I set up my growth engine?

Let's take a closer look at these questions:

1. Where is my growth going to come from?

There's no point optimizing your growth engine until you're clear about the opportunity you're going after. That means investing in sound analysis to identify where the growth is today and where it will be tomorrow, whether that's in your current sector or an adjacent one. Top growth leaders, once armed with a realistic picture of their company's growth situation, take care to set their priorities in the corporate mission, knowing growth initiatives can easily misfire if they aren't anchored in strategic business priorities. In some cases, companies will articulate or refine their corporate mission and vision in line with what they learn about growth in their industry.

Leaders map a view of their growth initiatives across two dimensions:

- **Scanning for growth opportunities.** This involves understanding how your industry and category is structured, how customers navigate it, where the profit pools are, and what trends are emerging. Then you figure out how your portfolio stacks up against it all. When one leading global consumer-goods company analyzed a set of critical factors—projected market size, proportion of nonloyal shoppers, and ability to convert consumers—it identified untapped value pools worth almost $100 million. Based on this analysis, it created a pipeline to tackle white spaces and new segments.

- **Getting granular with customer segmentation.** Our research on revenue growth at large companies suggests that executives should "de-average" their view of markets and develop a granular perspective on trends, future growth rates, and market structures. Insights into subindustries, segments, categories, micromarkets, and even pockets of growth within existing large accounts are the building blocks of portfolio choice and a critical factor in making sound decisions about where to compete. In the past few years, the use of advanced analytics to track behavior and preferences has made it possible to segment markets down to the level of individual customers. By pursuing mass personalization at scale, companies can lift revenues 5 to 15 percent while also improving the efficiency of their marketing spend and reducing acquisition costs.

One car-rental company used advanced data-mining techniques to analyze its database of driver profiles and trips. Having identified ten distinct customer archetypes, it pulled in data from external sources to build a scoring model that it used to identify drivers in a given city or neighborhood who fit one of these archetypes. By tailoring offers and communications to individual archetypes, it managed to grow its customer base by more than 10 percent in a year, increasing revenues by almost 20 percent.

2. How do I grow now and tomorrow?

Every growth journey is different, but there are three broad fronts: Invest, Perform, and Create. *Investing* in growth is something companies can start doing immediately by diverting funds from activities that are not performing efficiently or effectively into the right opportunities. *Performing* optimally in commercial functions allows companies to generate new revenues from growth in the medium term. And *creating* new offerings and business models custom-designed to satisfy unmet needs more completely, quickly, and flexibly than before enables companies to build a pipeline that fuels growth far into the future. The best companies use a combination of these three approaches to drive growth quickly, and reinvest released funds into future opportunities to support longer-term growth.

Invest: Put your money where the growth is

Large companies can capture significant incremental revenue through a relentless search for efficiencies and then reallocating those resources to promising new initiatives or proven winners. McKinsey research shows that "dynamic reallocators"—companies that reallocate at least 49 percent of the previous year's budget—achieve a compound annual growth rate of 10 percent in total return to shareholders (TRS). By contrast, "static allocators" that simply adjust last year's spending achieve TRS growth of just 6.1 percent.   Within 20 years, the dynamic reallocator will be worth twice as much as its less agile counterpart—a lead that is likely only to increase as digital disruption and geopolitical uncertainty make nimble reallocation even more important.

Central to this Invest approach is a thorough and rigorous approach to rooting out savings and a disciplined method of funneling funds to short- and long-term growth opportunities. Successful growth leaders have robust metrics and processes for identifying areas where they can squeeze out cost and a clear idea of where to invest every incremental dollar they find to drive growth.

Companies with the right mind-set can release tens or even hundreds of millions of dollars for reinvestment in a matter of months by optimizing their commercial functions. Savings can be captured from many sources, such as general and administrative expenses, but marketing is a prime candidate. Many companies can save 10 to 20 percent of their marketing budgets by making processes leaner and more efficient, paying the right price for a given service (and paying only for what they really need), and figuring out who does the work. By breaking open the black box around agency fees, for example, companies can save money and improve agility and quality. By optimizing consumer promotions and engagement (CPE) through better targeting, simpler programs, and better measurement, they can save 10 to 30 percent of their marketing spend.

Tracking marketing return on investment (MROI) helps companies identify underperforming marketing spend that can be reallocated to activities that deliver a better return on investment. Advanced analytics allows companies to measure the impact on customer behavior of offers and messages across multiple channels by combining media-mix modeling with digital-attribution modeling.

One European online retailer attracted 12 percent more active customers after reallocating internal and external resources, expanding its ecosystem of partners, and applying agile marketing approaches. It also implemented a customer-reactivation and -acquisition program and applied more rigor to MROI. Taken together, these initiatives enabled the retailer to raise its original growth target by a factor of six.

Perform: Optimize your commercial capabilities

Great growth companies constantly optimize their commercial capabilities in marketing, sales, pricing, and promotions. This approach helps to get much more growth from existing capabilities while also generating more revenue that can then be invested in growth opportunities.

Customer experience (CX) is one potent driver of growth. Successful CX enhancements can increase sales, facilitate cross-selling, and boost revenues by as much as 15 to 20 percent. One large European bank digitized its credit processes to slash its approval times for small and medium-sized enterprises (SMEs) lending from 20 days to less than ten minutes, far outpacing competitors. It increased win rates by a third and improved average margins by more than 50 percent.   Similarly, reducing the complexity of CX—for instance, by optimizing online self-help features such as FAQ pages so that customers don't have to make unnecessary calls to call centers—can free up savings in cost to serve on the order of 15 to 50 percent.

Introducing automated algorithm-driven dynamic pricing is another important source of growth. Companies can achieve sustainable price increases without damaging customer satisfaction by focusing resources on specific groups, such as more-profitable customers. Some global retail and consumer companies have achieved sales growth of 2 to 5 percent by this route, while also adding 5 to 10 percent to margins.   B2B businesses are adopting dynamic pricing too. After introducing a mix of new pricing approaches, redesigning its supporting organization and incentives, and training more than 300 frontline-sales staff, one global chemicals company achieved $150 million per year in incremental revenue over three years.

Similar growth opportunities exist in sales. Adopting omnichannel sales and analytics can be a crucial enabler of growth for B2B companies that understand when and when not to use digital. These companies achieve five times more revenue than their peers, eight times more operating profit, and twice the return to shareholders.   Adopting new digital channels can reduce the cost to acquire a new customer and the cost to serve an existing one, changing the commercial efficiency of the future channels that can be reinvested into current or new opportunities. From our research and experience, three traits have emerged that should be core ingredients of every company's optimal human-digital blend: speed, transparency, and expertise.

Create: Innovate by design with the customer at the center

To build things that customers want, a business needs to out-innovate its competitors—not just uncovering unmet customer needs to find profitable white spaces but also using technology to enter new markets or go to market in new ways. Yet a recent McKinsey survey found that just 27 percent of companies systematically scan for opportunities to expand beyond their core business.

New sources of growth come from redesigning business models, creating something new, and exploring disruptive services. New business models don't have to be complex; they could involve tapping into new sales channels to reach different customers, for instance, or introducing new services to support an existing product.

When exploring new opportunities, winners go beyond standard focus groups and surveys and pull in data on macro trends, marketplace analyses, ground-level performance metrics, and a host of other sources. Thanks to digitally enabled techniques such as social listening, sentiment analysis, digital ethnography, and online-consumer cocreation, research into unmet needs is more effective, more flexible, and faster than ever before. Companies can assemble an online focus group of B2B buyers in as little as ten minutes. Mobile ethnographies can be completed in a weekend; quantitative surveys can be fielded and analyzed in days.

Having equipped themselves with a deep understanding of customer purchase journeys, leading companies employ design thinking to create new products and services that will address unmet needs, reach unserved segments, or support entry into adjacent markets. At a time when consumers can choose from the best products that global marketplaces have to offer, design has become a key source of differentiation and a C-suite topic. Companies with scores in the top quartile of the McKinsey Design Index outperformed industry-benchmarked growth by as much as two to one.

To help get ideas to market quickly, winning innovators increasingly rely on "speedboats": small launches where a product is tested and refined in a real market setting. One global consumer-goods company has been testing products in nontraditional locations such as office buildings, juice shops, and yoga studios to gain insight into why consumers buy or don't buy them. Through multiple iterations, it uses the feedback to refine products until it sees indicators of success and then rapidly scales them. Today's companies can capitalize on this kind of approach because they have multiple distribution channels, digital channels, and social-media outlets at their disposal to reach consumers at low cost. They can also take advantage of external networks that support efficient and productive discovery and development.

The ability to scale up rapidly is critical to getting new products to market before competitors can. Leading consumer-goods innovators have reaped substantial rewards by scanning the market for promising ideas, watching for emerging consumer acceptance and new behaviors, and then jumping in before the market landscape has fully evolved. When we evaluated 25 high-growth categories in four countries in North and South America, Asia, and Europe, we found that companies that took this approach were growing faster than the market 60 to 80 percent of the time; in the US, they won the highest market share 80 percent of the time.

Merger & acquisition (M&A) functions can play an important role as well, though they need to become much more dynamic on reading the evolution of market trends, competitor moves, and the entry of new attackers. This requires greater focus on the return on capital in the current business areas and on future growth opportunities, and oftentimes an ecosystem of partners to deliver.

3. How do I set up my growth engine?

Markets shift, so businesses must keep finding and pursuing new sources of growth. To do that, they need a growth engine: an operating model underpinned by analytics and top talent, and built around the core blocks of organization-wide alignment, focused capability building, an agile culture, and a leadership mind-set.

To launch a growth transformation, the most important element will be dedicating sufficient resources and being rigorous in driving the process. That means putting in place a well-supported growth-transformation office that has the authority and resources to rigorously track and manage the transformation. It establishes a baseline and manages output to that baseline. This kind of central resource is crucial because it can drive and coordinate change across the entire business. It also provides a stable backbone with well-oiled processes for tracking implementation, driving initiatives, removing barriers, and managing trade-offs for short-term earnings targets. Without a dedicated team in place, change tends to be piecemeal or incremental, which inevitably leads to impact far below expectations.

The transformation office has an important role in focusing on developing the right capabilities. McKinsey research has found that top growers beat their peers by differentiating themselves in key capabilities such as data and analytics, and by developing products, services, and processes such as agile working and cross-functional collaboration.   In developing those growth capabilities, our research has shown that it's crucial to sequence their development thoughtfully. If you are moving from the bottom to the third quartile, for example, you might focus on aligning priority markets, building a product strategy and portfolio, and systematically measuring the voice of your consumer. If you move from the second to the top quartile, some examples of capabilities to develop include improving core offerings, introducing innovation awards, or improving processes to shorten commercialization cycles.

Developing these capabilities clearly has implications for talent and skills. Recent research by the McKinsey Global Institute found that digitization and automation are beginning to make new demands on workforce skills, with marketing and sales likely to be among the functions most affected. Up to 40 percent of sales activities can be automated with today's technology, and that number can go up to 50 percent as technology advances. Overall, the greatest need will be for advanced technological capabilities and basic digital skills, followed by social and emotional skills.

For new capabilities to take full effect, businesses need to reinvent how work gets done. That means making offices more like workshops, with employees working together to build something great. A McKinsey survey reported that 71 percent of high-growth companies have adopted agile processes such as scrum, sprints, cross-functional collaboration, and colocated teams.

Agile ways of working need to become a fact of life, embedded in every aspect of a company's operating model from innovation and product development through to marketing. Indeed, agile approaches are critical in enabling companies to target micro-markets, test ideas at speed, run hundreds of campaigns simultaneously, personalize offers on a truly granular scale, use data to drive decisions, and maximize MROI. This applies to embedding design thinking into how companies work. One major European furniture manufacturer employed both a central design department and small independent design teams working within product groups. It found the distributed teams had a clearer focus on customers and better cross-functional partnerships. They were 30 percent more successful in getting concepts to market and 10 percent faster in time to launch.

The final piece of the growth puzzle is a leadership mind-set. Top growth leaders are obsessed with growth and committed to keeping their business on a growth trajectory. They have a key role in developing a well-crafted story to help people at all levels understand what changes are in store, what the company is striving to create, and how new ways of working will affect what they do every day. Then they must communicate that clearly and continuously to the organization. They are also disciplined in the way they go about orienting the business to growth, constantly asking themselves and their peers questions such as:

- Do I use language that emphasizes growth rather than productivity?

- Do I and my top team role model the behavior we want to see from our employees?

- Should I carve out a lighthouse organization that focuses purely on growth?

Growth today drives not just performance, but survival itself. The companies with the brightest prospects are those that know where to find pockets of growth, how to capture that growth now and in the future, and how to build a growth engine for sustainable success.

From lab to leader: How consumer companies can drive growth at scale with disruptive innovation

In the era of "fast products" and digital disruption, delivering growth requires putting in place new predictive consumer-growth capabilities, including innovation, based on speed, agility, and scale.

Innovation is central to the mission, values, and agenda of most consumer-packaged-goods (CPG) companies. However, in the last several years, incumbent CPGs have struggled to keep pace with start-ups, which have reinvigorated and reinvented categories ranging from ice cream to diapers.

Our analysis of the food and beverage market from 2013–17 reveals that the top 25 manufacturers are responsible for 59 percent of sales but only 2 percent of category growth. Conversely, 44 percent of category growth has come from the next 400 manufacturers. Our experience in working with large consumer companies suggests that they don't suffer from a lack of ideas; where they struggle is in knowing where to make bets, moving products quickly to launch, and then nurturing them to scale. Effectively driving growth through innovation requires CPG companies to evolve many of the assets and capabilities already in place and adopt significantly different and new ways of working.

This change will not be easy. Many of the innovation systems that need to evolve are deeply entrenched. They have their own brand names, dedicated IT systems, firmly established management routines, and more. However, our work with CPG organizations has convinced us that these changes are necessary and can return significant value. Our analysis of ~350 CPG companies across 21 subcategories found that growth leaders excelled at harnessing commercial capabilities, including innovation. Additional McKinsey analysis has shown that CPG "Creator" companies—those that consistently develop new products or services—grow more than their peers. These winning Creators have adopted a formula that borrows the best from progressive new players while fully leveraging existing advantages in scope and scale.

How did we get here?

For the past two decades, CPG innovation models have been designed to maintain and steadily grow already at-scale brands. This meant that most innovations were largely incremental moves with the occasional one-off disruptive success. This slow and steady approach worked because CPGs didn't really need disruptive innovation to grow. Geographic expansion, pricing, and brand extensions were all successful strategies that kept the top line moving. As a result, most of the systems designed to manage these innovations were optimized for fairly predictable and low-volatility initiatives. They emphasized reliability and risk management.

That very success, however, led to calcified thinking as companies built large brands and poured resources into supporting and protecting them. In recent years, as they have tried to respond to new entrants and rapidly changing consumer needs, CPGs found their innovation systems tended to stifle and stall more disruptive efforts. As the returns from innovation dwindled, companies cut marketing, insights, and innovation budgets to cover profit shortfalls. This created a negative cycle. As a stopgap, many large consumer companies have turned to M&A to fill holes in the innovation portfolio—but on its own, M&A can be a very expensive path to growth with its own difficulties in scalability and cultural fit.

How new upstarts "do" innovation—speed, agility, consumer-first—is not exactly a secret. Many CPGs have made concerted efforts to embrace those attributes by setting up incubators, garages, or labs. They have tried to become agile and use test-and-learn programs. But while there have been notable successes, they tend to be episodic or fail to scale because they happen at the periphery of the main innovation system, or even as explicit "exemptions" from standard processes. Scaled success requires making disruptive innovation part of the normal course of business.

What to learn from today's innovators

Despite the many challenges, there are consumer companies winning in the market and driving profitable growth. Here are four shifts they're making:

1. Focus on targeted consumer needs.

All of us can think of innovative products that are competing head to head in established categories (some of our favorites include Halo Top, SkinnyPop, and Blue Buffalo). A common denominator for most of them is that they didn't start big but focused instead on a targeted and unmet consumer need that turned out to have broad reach.

That approach stands in stark contrast to the standard CPG model, where companies look for the products that satisfy the largest group ("gen pop"). An important reason for this focus is that many CPGs need an idea to be big enough to make a dent in their business. They also look to get the highest ROI for innovations to amortize the high costs historically required to launch (especially ad campaigns and capital expenditures for new manufacturing). But in a world where it is less expensive and easier than ever for companies to address more targeted needs, and where consumers have never had more choices at their fingertips, gen pop is becoming less and less viable as an objective or requirement.

This isn't to suggest that large CPG firms should stop looking for large and growing opportunities. But the evidence is clear that there are plenty of products that start small and would normally be killed off at a large CPG company, that explode once in the market.

All strong innovation begins with the ability to identify a consumer need that the marketplace isn't addressing. That happens by:

- *Exploring granular consumer needs with advanced analytics.* CPG leaders explore opportunities through highly granular, data-rich maps of product benefits, consumer needs, and usage occasions rather than just segments or categories (we call these Growth Maps). These can reveal how a seemingly niche and emerging trend could have surprisingly broad reach and applicability.

- *Combining many data sources to quickly address tipping-point trends.* Leaders combine various data sources (consumer, business, technology) to identify market trends that are hitting relevant tipping points. They understand where the most promising trends are, where they have existing capabilities to play, and where they might need to build new muscle. And they bring all this together to rapidly prioritize where to take action.

- *Using design thinking.* By using empathy to uncover unspoken and unmet needs, designing new solutions with consumers and channel partners, and rapidly prototyping and testing, design thinking produces distinctive answers. Importantly, true design thinking continues to incorporate consumer insights and iterate product designs even after initial product launch (see more below). Two leading consumer companies in Japan recently set up "innovation garages" to integrate design thinking into product development methods. They were excited by the power of integrating design into product development methods to produce better, more consumer-driven products radically faster.

2. Launch more "speedboats"—accepting that some of them will sink.

There is a prevailing myth that consumer companies need to do a few big launches a year. Even if that were once true, it no longer is. This approach required large R&D investments, extensive consumer testing to validate willingness to purchase, and massive resources (large advertising, promotion, and distribution budgets)—all in an attempt to predict success and perfect a product before a large, potentially multicountry launch. This mentality assumed the resulting product could not fail once it hit the open market.

However, our findings suggest that putting all this effort and funding to drive a successful launch has not actually provided the desired results. In packaged food, for example, a review of new brands and disruptive innovations launched in 2013 by large CPG companies found that only 25 percent were still around four years later. This success rate is no better than what start-ups and small CPGs achieved with much smaller budgets and programs (Exhibit 1).

Exhibit 1

The 'few big bets' approach by large incumbents has not improved outcomes—winning requires getting more products successfully into market.

Packaged food, US, 2013-17

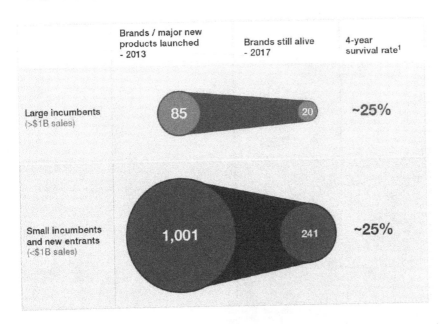

	Brands / major new products launched - 2013	Brands still alive - 2017	4-year survival rate[1]
Large incumbents (>$1B sales)	85	20	~25%
Small incumbents and new entrants (<$1B sales)	1,001	241	~25%

[1] Based on brands available and fulfilled by Amazon in Aug 2017 and/or recognized by market reports as share leaders

Winning innovators, in contrast, increasingly rely on speedboats: smaller launches where the product is tested and refined in-market. Take the example of one global CPG that is extensively using "first-purchase testing" to understand why consumers are/are not purchasing a product, then integrating that feedback into further iterations (Exhibit 2). It has been testing real products in multiple nontraditional settings including office buildings, juice shops, and yoga studios. The insights gained from these live settings allow the company to rapidly iterate the product design. Once indicators of success are seen, it moves to rapidly scale the product via Amazon and traditional retailers. The approach works, because in today's ecosystem, there are many distribution channels and digital and social-media outlets to reach consumers less expensively, as well as external networks that can support efficient and productive discovery and development.

Exhibit 2

Leaders work differently within and across four distinct phases for breakthrough success.

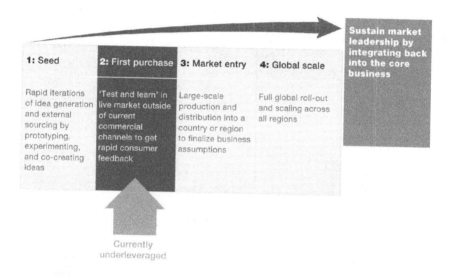

The Internet also provides an under-utilized testing ground for speedboats. Many disruptive brands start by marketing direct to consumers, which allows them to hone the product and messaging, while capturing detailed data on purchase behavior. Even without e-commerce, most start-ups are heavily using social media like Facebook to reach targeted audiences with lower cost and risk.

More speedboats, however, can mean more headaches for general managers who have to keep track of more projects and then nurture products to scale. CPG leaders address this through strong portfolio management. They make clear, prioritized choices about the categories and segments in which they will innovate and which ones they will maintain or exit from. They put in place clear processes for tracking performance and new allocation mechanisms to quickly get funds to promising programs. And when they need to scale new bets, they fund them by reinvesting initial proceeds from the speedboats.

3. Think (and act) like a venture investor.

Traditional stage gate processes are very efficient for managing a large pipeline of similar ideas through a relatively standard development pathway. However, when they are used for more disruptive initiatives, they tend to systematically smother or starve them. A different system is required for disruptive innovation.

Consider how venture-capital firms manage their portfolio of investments. They analyze each investment on its own merits, adapting as businesses evolve. They couple funding closely to the progress of the new business and meet at the speed of its progress versus on a predefined calendar. The hurdle rates and KPIs are also different, with emphasis on whether they are gaining consumer traction in addition to improving financials. And more than anything, they are relentless in pushing the pace and urgency of growth.

To deliver on this capability, we often recommend that companies establish their own venture board comprising their strongest leaders. Even though the scale may be small, this is some of the hardest work in the company and the most important to its future. Along with a few outsiders to inject a more objective perspective, this board is responsible for maximizing the return of the more aggressive portfolio—and has complete autonomy to quickly make decisions about it.

4. First to scale beats first to market.

Launching disruptive innovation doesn't mean a company always has to be the original inventor. Rather than focusing on first to market, we recommend focusing on first to scale. We found that leading CPG innovators who actively scan the market for high-potential ideas, watch for emerging consumer acceptance and new behaviors, and then jump in before the market landscape has fully evolved have reaped significant rewards. We evaluated 25 high-growth categories in four countries across North and South America, Asia, and Europe. In each, the players who took this approach are winning ~60 to 80 percent of the time; in the US, they win the highest market share 80 percent of the time.

Incumbent CPGs can turn to their ingrained advantages to identify and scale these ideas. Their wealth of consumer data can be used to spot trends earlier than others. Their significant financial and human resources can be disproportionately allocated to hot opportunities. The distribution and account relationships incumbents have across multiple retailers can be used to expand the market for new products more easily and quickly than new players with a smaller network of relationships. Large CPGs are also attractive partners for innovators with insightful ideas but insufficient resources to develop and scale them.

All of the above are incumbents' advantages that many smaller players would love to acquire. Using these advantages to their fullest requires CPGs to adopt a much stronger orientation toward speed, nurture more disruptive bets until they can be scaled, and reallocate resources to the strongest opportunities.

How to get started

Embracing the above shifts will require meaningful changes. In our experience, the changes are not only eminently achievable, but also reenergize the organization as they make innovation and delighting consumers more central and less cumbersome to accomplish. We recommend CPG leaders do five things now:

1. Address the culture.

senior executive team. As one consumer executive—who grew her company to a billion-dollar valuation in less than 15 years—put it, "Innovation is simply everyone's job. . . . Everyone is expected to look for insights, to bring ideas, to be ready to help drive an initiative." Other ingredients include: a near-maniacal focus on the consumer—by which we mean putting the consumer at the center of every decision; incentives to reward innovation; metrics that track innovation—consumer excitement, word of mouth, adoption rates; and a clear understanding of how each person's role adds value to the process. Reward learning and make learnings easily available and easy to share.

2. Create high aspirations and hard metrics.

"Let's increase growth by 2 to 3 percent!" That kind of aspiration won't motivate people and drive new thinking. Contrast that rather vague hope with this one from a mining (!) company: "Generate $150 million of incremental EBITDA over the next five years by discovering new applications for our products, moving closer to our end customers, and leading our industry in production processes." This is bold, actionable, measurable, and gives teams some sense of where and how they should innovate. To track progress against aspirations, metrics need to be specific, of course, but they also need to evolve. For example, metrics on market share or growth rate will be better in the earlier phase of a product's lifecycle. Shift the focus to value and margin as the project scales and matures. Metrics also must be in the business-unit (BU) leader's performance objectives.

3. Define the hunting grounds.

Make clear choices about where you will innovate. Be careful to define them by working backward from the consumers and markets you serve rather than the way you currently define your brand and category structures, particularly in multibrand organizations. Too often we see outdated guardrails unnecessarily limit brands from exploring new spaces. As one CEO, whose company was acquired by a leading global CPG incumbent, put it, "If your consumers want your brand to move into a space and you don't, then rest assured someone else will."

4. Reallocate resources.

In our experience, most incumbent CPGs have too many resources committed to initiatives that are unlikely to drive meaningful growth. The first step in liberating resources is to take a hard look at the portfolio and reallocate people to more aggressive growth opportunities. Crucially, this cannot be an annual or even quarterly exercise. Leading innovators continually and ruthlessly reallocate resources and make sure scarce people and dollars are put to the best use. As one innovative CPG leader in Asia Pacific said, "I established three simple mandates: bigger (more top-line potential), better (more differentiated), and faster (time to market)." These mandates drove top-line growth at four to five times the underlying category growth.

5. Put a new disruptive innovation "system" in place based on agile models.

Driving success at scale requires a new model. Innovative ideas can initially generate a lot of excitement and promise. But that drive often wilts when it needs to work with the full business to scale the idea. While there is a broad range of elements in a new innovation system, we find that the following are a few of the most important:

- *Establish cross-functional teams with a complementary set of problem-solving skills,* such as people from insights, marketing, personnel, sales, UX, and tech. The team should "live" together, using an agile development model, and ideally drive one to two initiatives at any given time.

- *Focus on constant learning and de-risking throughout development.* Rather than a standard checklist of activities and stages, teams should constantly identify and prioritize the greatest uncertainties in a concept and conduct quick tests to resolve them.

- *Set up and prequalify your "speedboat" network.* These can be factories, partners, agencies, and vendors who can support small-scale procurement and manufacturing, run first-purchase tests, and even support a riskier new product's first few years of manufacturing before committing the capital expenditure for scaled/global manufacturing.

- **_Hardwire points of contact between the innovation labs and the "mother ship."_** Embed people from the sponsor BU as a core part of the innovation team, and rotate people from the main business through the innovation labs. Assign respected leaders from the legacy business to manage innovation projects. Create a central innovation roadmap that business units agree on, and track it on the CEO/COO agenda.

The growth game has changed, but that doesn't mean that CPG companies can't change with it. With a commitment to new mind-sets and approaches, CPG companies can harness speed and agility to move again to the forefront of innovation.

Debunking four myths of organic growth

New analysis reveals corporate blind spots when it comes to driving growth.

While **organic growth** is crucial to a company's survival, many executives underestimate its value. In past research, we found that fewer than 30 percent of businesses systematically scan for and evaluate new growth opportunities.   The reasons for this vary from reliance on cost-cutting efforts to difficulty overcoming short-term pressures.

To better understand how the best-growing companies achieve their success, we asked respondents to our newest McKinsey Global Survey on growth how their companies develop proficiency and expertise along three dimensions, or lenses, of organic growth.
Companies can **Invest**, or identify pockets of growth and reallocate resources to them; they can **Create**, or innovate products, services, and business models; and they can **Perform**, or excel at commercial functions and operations.   The results from our top-growth companies —that is, the companies where respondents report revenue growth four or more percentage points higher than the industry growth rate—appear to debunk some commonly held myths about organic growth and what it takes to do it well.

Myth 1: Creating new products, services, and businesses is the best way to grow

It's easy for executives to get swept up in the excitement of launching a new product or service, and it's tempting for companies to focus only on developing new products, services, or business models (Create) as the primary way to grow organically. But the data suggest that top-growth companies tend to follow a different approach.

In fact, a majority of respondents at top-growth companies say they grow primarily through the other two lenses, with 44 percent reporting a primary focus on identifying and reallocating resources (Invest) toward growth (Exhibit 1).   It makes sense that top-growth companies adopt this lens more often than the other two, given that the most common best practices for investing all relate to how a company fundamentally focuses its resources and organizational attention on growth. These practices include establishing goals for growth that set the agenda throughout the organization, making investment decisions based on systematic evaluations of returns, and leadership alignment on market strategy.

Exhibit 1

Top growers often have a strong command of performance-related data and analytics.

Primary lens[1] of top-quartile growth companies
% of respondents at top-growth companies[2]

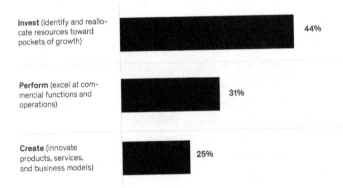

Invest (identify and reallo-cate resources toward pockets of growth)	44%
Perform (excel at commercial functions and operations)	31%
Create (innovate products, services, and business models)	25%

[1]A company's primary lens is based on the highest number of best practices within each one that respondents agreed or strongly agreed with. For Invest, the survey asked about 7 practices; for Perform, 8 practices; and for Create, 6 practices.
[2]Respondents who said their company's annual growth rate in the past 3 years has been at least 4 percent higher than the overall growth rate of their sector; n = 426.

Furthermore, the results suggest that organizations are better positioned for growth when they develop a broad set of complementary capabilities. Building sets of capabilities that reinforce each other—that is, adopting best practices in two or three lenses—is associated with dramatically higher odds of being a top-growth company (Exhibit 2).

Exhibit 2

According to the survey results, mastering multiple lenses dramatically improves company growth rates.

Companies' annual growth rates relative to their sector's
past 3 years, percentage-point difference

Mastery is defined as respondents' agreement that their companies are effective or very effective at 70 percent or more of practices in a given lens. For Invest, the survey asked about 7 practices; for Perform, 8 practices; and for Create, 8 practices. At companies that have mastered no lenses, n = 765; at companies that have mastered 1, n = 320; and at companies that have mastered 2 or 3, n = 381.

But organizations should exercise caution before pursuing all three lenses at once. Only 12 percent of respondents say their companies have successfully mastered all three, suggesting that mastery of these lenses requires a level of organizational attention and investment that few companies are currently able to meet.

Corning's two-decade transformation into an innovation powerhouse illustrates the effectiveness of a dual-pronged Invest/Create approach. In 2002, the company was in crisis: the dot-com bubble had burst, sapping demand for the fiber-optic cabling that had been the source of nearly all its profits. In 2001, Corning posted a $5.5 billion net loss, nearly equal to their revenues.

To come back from the brink, the company pulled Invest levers. It squeezed the business to preserve cash, slashing payrolls by half, and pivoted the remaining cash toward the budding LCD market to create near-term profitable growth. Freeing up that capital let the company start investing in R&D (Create)—reaching 11 percent of sales in 2004—to capture new opportunities such as ceramic filters for diesel engines. That Create competency positioned them, in 2007, to answer Steve Jobs' call to develop millions of square feet of 1.3-mm, ultrastrong glass within six months. Revenues from the resulting Gorilla Glass skyrocketed to $700 million by 2012. In 2015, Corning codified this virtuous Invest/Create cycle as the Strategy and Capital Allocation framework, which is still functioning today.

The company has continued to focus on this model. From 2011–16 (the last dates for which we have figures), it slated $10 billion, equivalent to a full year's revenue, for investment in R&D, capital spending, and strategic acquisitions.

Myth 2: What worked before will work going forward

For companies looking for growth, it can be tempting to double down on what worked in the past. The reality is, however, that companies need to build new strengths in order to continue growing.

The survey's results indicate that, across industries, a few common capabilities support a pathway to organic growth. In other words, companies can focus on developing the capabilities that will address the biggest hurdles impeding their growth performance at a given point in time (Exhibit 3).

Exhibit 3

The results suggest that companies should focus on building different capabilities at different stages of their growth performance.

Capabilities for moving to next level of organic growth, relative to industry's average growth rate

● Ranked in top 5[1]

	From growth below industry rate to industry-rate growth	From industry-rate growth to growth just above industry rate[2]	From growth just above industry rate[2] to top grower[3]
Invest			
Leaders are aligned on market strategy	●		
Pipeline of next-generation products/services is actively managed	●		●
Portfolio management decisions are based on evaluations of returns		●	
Resources are rapidly reallocated to high-growth-potential investments		●	
Growth goals are managed top-down		●	
Create			
New products/services are developed to address unmet needs	●		
Budget includes development of disruptive business models/offerings		●	
Small failures are accepted as necessary and important to innovation			●
Employees feel safe and encouraged to take calculated risks			●
Perform			
Customer feedback is used systematically to adjust offerings	●		●
Focus of growth strategy is high-profit/high-growth-potential customers	●		
Centers of excellence are dedicated to advanced capabilities		●	
There is a consistent effort to shorten commercialization cycles			●

[1] That is, the capabilities with largest percentage-point differences in shares of respondents at each level who agree that the capability is present in their company. The survey asked about 91 capabilities in total.
[2] Respondents who said their company's annual growth rate in the past 3 years has been 1 to 3 percent higher than the overall growth rate of their sector; n = 318.
[3] Respondents who said their company's annual growth rate in the past 3 years has been at least 4 percent higher than the overall growth rate of their sector; n = 426.

Companies growing slower than their industries, for instance, should focus on improving the fit between the market and their products, by addressing unmet customer needs and systematically acting on customer feedback, for example, to catch up to the industry growth rate. To grow faster than the industry average, they should also establish a stronger foundation of resource-allocation capabilities, perhaps by transferring resources from underperforming investments to those with greater growth potential. Once organizations are growing above the industry average, in order to maximize growth, they should focus their efforts in the ways that have proven successful for top-growth companies by:

- pursuing innovation through short commercialization cycles (58 percent of top-growth respondents, compared with 44 percent of those growing only slightly faster than their industry average)

- actively managing their product and service pipeline (67 percent, compared with 55 percent)

- accepting small failures as necessary and important to innovation (07 percent, compared with 41 percent)

Before 2012, Adobe leaned heavily on Perform capabilities,   increasing pricing and squeezing as much additional revenue as possible out of its physically boxed products. But Perform capabilities could only bring it so far. After seeing sales drop by 20 percent during the recession, Adobe began exploring other models to strengthen its financial buffer and better serve customers' rapidly changing needs.

Tapping into a combination of Create and Invest capabilities, the organization built pricing and uptake models, analyzed return on investment (ROI), and ultimately landed on the software-asa-service (SaaS) model. After aligning leadership through several experiments offering both subscription and perpetual-licensing models, Adobe announced the "Creative Cloud" in late 2011 and immediately shifted resources and investments to this online suite of products. By May 2013, leadership pulled resources from building out the perpetual-licensing product and put the entire organization behind the subscription model.

This shift to the cloud proved fruitful for Adobe. By the end of 2017, the company had seen three consecutive years of double-digit revenue growth and recurring revenue was 84 percent of total revenue with an estimated 12 million subscribers.

Myth 3: Innovation capabilities can't be developed

For companies that have built a strong foundation of capabilities, creating innovative products and business models can be a powerful and differentiating source of growth. In fact, among the three lenses, Create is the one in which respondents at top-growth companies report the largest gap between themselves and their nearest peers.

But realizing growth through innovation can feel as elusive as it is important: it requires exceptional creativity and can bring about transformational results. Of the creation-related capabilities we asked about, top-growth respondents most often say their companies accept small failures as a necessary part of innovation, which is also the practice that most differentiates these companies from those growing just above the industry rate (Exhibit 4). They also report a much higher tolerance for employee risk taking than their peers.

Exhibit 4

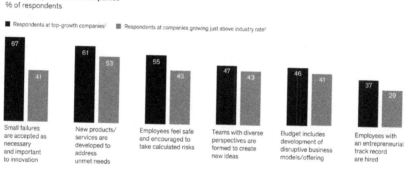

Among the top growers' strongest capabilities for Create is accepting small failures as necessary to innovation.

'Create' capabilities at companies[1]
% of respondents

■ Respondents at top-growth companies[2]   ■ Respondents at companies growing just above industry rate[3]

67	61	55	47	46	37
41	53	43	43	41	29
Small failures are accepted as necessary and important to innovation	New products/ services are developed to address unmet needs	Employees feel safe and encouraged to take calculated risks	Teams with diverse perspectives are formed to create new ideas	Budget includes development of disruptive business models/offering	Employees with an entrepreneurial track record are hired

[1]Respondents who said their company is effective or very effective at each practice.
[2]Respondents who said their company's annual growth rate in the past 3 years has been at least 4 percent higher than the overall growth rate of their sectors; n = 426.
[3]Respondents who said their company's annual growth rate in the past 3 years has been 1 to 3 percent higher than the overall growth rate of their sectors; n = 313.

The experience of Tyson Foods' postcrisis turnaround illustrates how a business can develop effective Create capabilities. The CEO made a commitment to product innovation, instituting a "trends council" to systematically connect consumer-research findings to each business

51

function, staffing mixed-background innovator teams to build product pipelines, and doubling R&D spend over four years. Beyond specific tactics, the leadership team worked to create a pervasive culture that encouraged risk taking and new frontiers.

They enabled that Create lens with complementary Perform capabilities: they used pricing to carefully position their innovations in four growth platforms; in distribution, they diversified into e-commerce; in operations, they staffed industry experts on their innovator teams. Through these efforts, the organization was able to build a diverse portfolio of category-leading brands. From 2012–16, Tyson produced 2 percent real, organic, top-line growth annually in a marketplace that grew only 0.3 percent annually, while at the same time expanding its margins by nearly four percentage points.

Myth 4: Superior growth is not possible in my industry

It is well known that a sector's overall growth is correlated with the growth rates of individual companies within it.   But that reality can become a crutch for underperforming companies, especially in slow-growth sectors. When the idea that best-practice growth capabilities are hard or even futile to develop is a pervasive mind-set, it becomes an additional barrier to acting on and addressing growth.

The data, however, tell a different story. On average, respondents across industries report very similar rates of adopting key growth capabilities— between 40 and 50 percent, whether they are in high tech or in basic materials.

Furthermore, the results indicate that top-growth companies exist in every industry. When comparing the capabilities of top-growth companies with those of companies growing below the industry rate, the results suggest a significant gap—between 20 and 46 percentage points—across sectors in the adoption of best practices (Exhibit 5). In other words, significant jumps in growth rates are possible in any industry when companies have strong organizational capabilities in place.

Exhibit 5

Across industries, respondents report a similar distribution of organizational capabilities for growth.

% of respondents reporting effective or very effective growth practices at their company

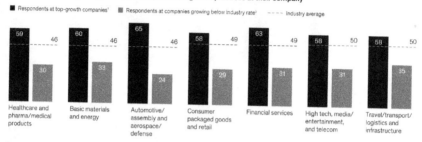

■ Respondents at top-growth companies¹   ■ Respondents at companies growing below industry rate²   ‑ ‑ ‑ ‑ Industry average

| Healthcare and pharma/medical products | Basic materials and energy | Automotive/ assembly and aerospace/ defense | Consumer packaged goods and retail | Financial services | High tech, media/ entertainment, and telecom | Travel/transport/ logistics and infrastructure |

¹Respondents who said their company's annual growth rate in the past 3 years has been at least 4 percent higher than the overall growth rate of their sector; n = 425.
²n = 299.

One industry that has seen slow top-line growth is specialty chemicals. Our previous analyses of the sector show that most of the increases in total return to shareholders (TRS) come from valuation increases and margin improvements, driven by functional excellence. One area where the industry has been less successful is in driving top-line growth.

The specialty-chemicals division of a major conglomerate set out to improve EBIT by more than three percentage points through revamping account-management capabilities. It created a program to segment and prioritize customers and to identify opportunities for cost reduction and margin leakage through internal analyses and benchmarks, then rolled out key-account action plans and best-practice commercial policies. The initial success within the pilot business unit led the organization to invest over 2,500 full-time employee hours into capability building across the corporation. After 12 months, the organization was on track to demonstrate top-line growth along with a ten point plus EBIT, three times higher than it had originally sought.

It's important for companies reviewing their growth agenda and strategizing for improvement to take a hard look at their explicit or implicit assumptions on how growth is achieved. Deliberate identification and targeting of capabilities is a tried-and-true method that distinguishes firms with consistent growth records from those without them.

A proven recipe for organic growth: Deliberate focus on a diversified approach

Companies, like people, tend to do what's worked well in the past. But when it comes to driving organic growth, that past success can often create "blind spots" and close off a vast range of opportunities. Being deliberate and focused on building a diversified growth program has proven much more effective. McKinsey's Barr Seitz recently sat down with Liz Hilton Segel, a senior partner in McKinsey's New York office and leader of the Marketing & Sales Practice in the Americas, to discuss the importance of corporate dexterity in driving organic growth in the digital age.

Why is it important to think in terms of multiple ways to drive organic growth?

We've done a lot of work with clients who are trying to change their growth trajectory and with private-equity owners who are evaluating whether to buy a new asset and whether that asset will be worth more over the long run.

What we've found is that there are really three different approaches companies take to try to increase their overall growth rate: they can Invest, Create, or Perform.

Executives tend to use strategies that worked for them in the past, which can reflect a personal preference or a specific company context. Either way, they tend to employ one technique more than the others.

Companies also face myriad distractions—cost agendas, regulations, or other business requirements. So part of what's required is a focus on growth and buy-in from the management team to growth as the top priority of the business. Once this foundation had been laid and everyone is committed, the question becomes how to accomplish the goal, and the work begins on laying out the roadmap to get there.

How does this Invest-Create-Perform approach help to achieve growth?

Let me share an example. We were engaged by a private-equity firm to evaluate whether an entertainment company in the theme-park space could generate greater growth. Our approach was classic due diligence, but we applied the Investor-Creator-Performer framework to our thinking.

On the Investor portion, our first question was, "How many new cities could absorb one of these theme parks?" We found that there were cities all over the world where the company could grow dramatically with some additional investment.

Then we scrutinized what the company's theme parks offered to patrons in the way of things like room types, available entertainment, and the bar and restaurant scene. We realized that some further innovation in their value proposition could ratchet their average daily revenue up significantly.

Finally, we examined their sales channels, which we found didn't have nearly the required level of performance management. So we introduced a very simple scorecard to track performance.

By applying the Investor-Creator-Performer framework, we learned they could achieve a very significant amount of top-line growth.

What are the main characteristics of a successful Investor strategy for driving growth?

Companies that pursue the Investor approach believe the way to get top-line revenue growth is to put more investment to work. They'll typically go after some form of a cost-savings program either in procurement or in selling, general and administrative expenses. They may also find incremental margins through pricing action.

They're looking to build a war chest and apply it to either growing their distribution channels, growing their sales force, or putting significant investment behind marketing. They'll know exactly what they're going to get for the next $10 million of investment in their sales force and have the confidence of a quantified return if they release incremental spending in their sales or marketing channel.

There's also a need to look across the company and identify parts that have both less and more opportunity for top-line growth and then make a purposeful reallocation of capital to enable the company to grow.

What capabilities or practices need to be in place for an Investor growth strategy to pay off?

We're finding that companies are moving to a much more dynamic investment-reallocation approach to fund growth possibilities, using new ideas about where to make incremental investments in either the sales force, new marketing programs, a new product line, or a new country.

One of my clients in the credit card industry employs an extremely disciplined process for marketing-investment allocation. They reevaluate the investment choices open to them on a monthly basis, making reallocation decisions according to available investment capacity at the time.

What amazes me is that companies pursuing an Investor growth strategy are ones where the CFO is usually arm-in-arm with either the CEO or the head of the business unit, really working in lockstep to change the company's trajectory. In companies where growth is not the priority, you'll typically see a finance organization or a CFO much more focused on cost containment and margins.

How do companies successfully pursue a Creator strategy to drive organic growth?

In companies with a Creator mind-set, there's a conviction and a belief that with the launch of a new product, new revenues will follow. But in companies that lack a Creator mind-set, there's a sense that existing products are going to have to deliver as they are, or a lack of belief in the possibility of a new product driving new revenues.

Digital is creating so many opportunities for companies to change how they engage with consumers and putting a real premium on the customer experience. If they invest behind a new customer experience—potentially a completely digitally enabled customer experience— that might give them the opportunity to shift their market position.

What does a Performer growth approach look like?

Growth Performers operate with a continuous-improvement mind-set. These are companies that look at their sales force and say, "I am 100 percent positive that with this exact same sales force I can find a way to new top-line growth."

It might mean deeper insights about which segments of the sales force can produce better returns or a greater understanding of the different industry segments that they're selling to. A company pursuing a Performer approach to growth often looks quite closely at pricing decisions and makes far more disciplined choices about where to provide discounting and where to take incremental price increases.

Companies that pursue the Performer approach to growth are literally able to generate a 5, 10, or 15 percent increase in their revenue production with the exact same investment in their sales and marketing engine.

What traits do CEOs who are most effective at driving growth in their businesses share?

CEOs who believe they can change the growth rate of their business usually focus both on the short term and the long term. So they'll be looking quite closely at results, let's say over the next six quarters. They'll be looking for programs they're confident can produce very visible results that can be reported to the analyst community and build a sense of momentum.

These CEOs generally set a very ambitious agenda around growth. They'll galvanize the whole team so everyone knows they share a single-minded purpose, which is to take the company on a top-line-growth journey. They typically set an agenda for growth just as a company going after a cost transformation would. They lay out a purposeful set of initiatives and put the investment path in place necessary to spur growth.

For example, one of my clients joined a company that had been consistently delivering on its earnings targets, but had not been delivering revenue growth on any material level for quite some time. During one of his first weeks, he took a look at all the company reports and noticed one of their call centers wasn't delivering the same performance level as the other three.

He picked up the phone and called the head of that call center and asked, "Why aren't you delivering at the level that we expect?" He would immediately get a bump in performance. So he called somebody who's three levels below him and said, "I've been looking at your close rate, and your close rate's four points below the other call centers'. What exactly is going on over there? I'd like to talk about it again next week." He sent a signal that said, "We're watching the performance of all of our sales and marketing channels very carefully."

The most perfect union: Unlocking the next wave of growth by unifying creativity and analytics

Companies that harness creativity and data in tandem have growth rates twice as high as companies that don't. Here's how they do it.

" I deas and numbers" have always had an uneasy alliance in marketing. To creative directors, designers, and copywriters, creativity is an instinctual process of building emotional bonds with consumers. Bring in too much quantitative analysis and the magic dies.

"[As marketers] we have to understand and connect with customers," the CMO of a hospitality company recently told McKinsey. "I'm afraid the data people will win, and it will all become a commodity if brand and creativity don't matter anymore. I'm afraid the creative process will lose its soul."

Despite such understandable concerns, the notion that creativity and data are adversaries is simply outdated. Combining the power of human ingenuity and the insights gleaned from data analytics is a good start. But the best marketers are going a step further and integrating this power combo into all functions across the marketing value chain—from brand strategy and consumer insights, to customer experience, product, and pricing to content and creative development, media—even measurement. Far from robbing a brand of its soul, this fusion of skills and mind-sets is an essential part of the modernization of marketing to drive growth.

As part of an ongoing series of studies in conjunction with the Cannes Lions Festival and the Association of National Advertisers, McKinsey recently surveyed more than 200 CMOs and senior marketing executives (including interviews with 25+ of the CMOs) and tracked the performance of their companies. We found that marketers who are what we call "integrators"—those who have united data and creativity—grow their revenues at twice the average rate of S&P 500 companies: at least 10 percent annually versus 5 percent (Exhibit 1). This is a welcome development for CMOs, who no longer see themselves primarily as stewards of the company's brand, but as drivers of company growth. One CMO told McKinsey that he has shifted the entire C-suite's view of marketing spend from a P&L expense to an investment the company is making in its future.

Exhibit 1

Marketers who integrate creativity and data drive more growth.

Data-driven creativity scores[1]

Scale of 1–5

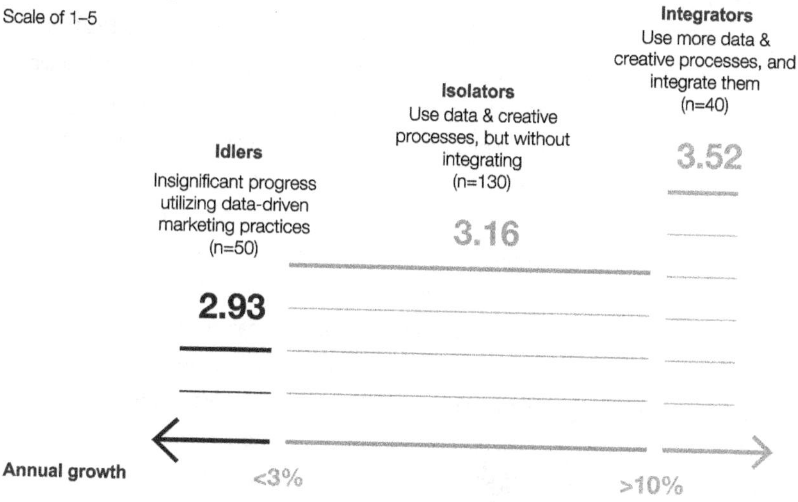

Integrators
Use more data &
creative processes, and
integrate them
(n=40)

Isolators
Use data & creative
processes, but without
integrating
(n=130)

Idlers
Insignificant progress
utilizing data-driven
marketing practices
(n=50)

3.52

3.16

2.93

Annual growth ← <3% >10% →

1. An index examining the level of integration between data and creativity within the marketing function

The study also revealed that while marketers rarely consider their creative output "world class" or "iconic," those integrators with the 10+ percent growth see their efforts as "engaging," "unique," and a core contributor to the creation of brand equity. Some go so far as to call their creative output a key part of what sets them apart from competitors.

Here are three distinct ways in which these integrators are modernizing marketing:

1. They treat creativity and data as equal partners.

In companies that are integrators, creative functions are becoming more data driven, and data-driven functions are growing more creative. Two areas where we see this happening most clearly are customer experience and consumer insights.

First, customer experience: Historically, this is a function overseen by people who think creatively and strategically about how to meet and exceed customer expectations. But today, data analytics can uncover customer intentions, triggers, and interests that reveal subtle pain points and unmet needs. We found that the integrators in our study continuously and rigorously mine for such insights as part of the day-to-day process of improving customer experience instead of using analytics in a separate, adjacent process (Exhibit 2). On average, they use four or more types of insights and analytic techniques, both traditional (focus groups, primary research, third-party research) and data driven (customer-journey analytics, advanced analytics, and artificial intelligence), whereas their non-integrator peers use three or fewer. A majority (70 percent) of integrators employ advanced analytics for consumer insights, compared with only 40 percent of companies with average growth. And 65 percent of integrators use customer-journey analytics, versus 50 percent of average growers. We call this latter category of companies "isolators" because, while they are using both data-driven and creative processes, they are doing so in isolation without integrating them across their marketing functions. The final category in our survey is "idlers": companies that are growing 3 percent a year or less and have made insignificant progress in utilizing data-driven marketing practices.

Exhibit 2

Integrators make better use of creativity and data than peers.

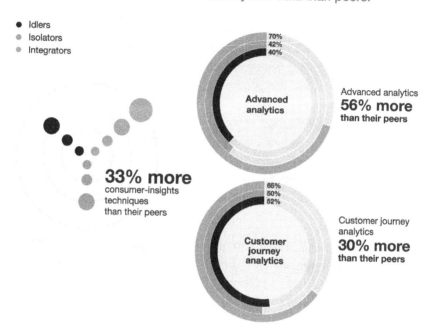

- Idlers
- Isolators
- Integrators

Advanced analytics
70%
42%
40%

Advanced
analytics

Advanced analytics
56% more
than their peers

33% more
consumer-insights
techniques
than their peers

65%
50%
52%

Customer
journey
analytics

Customer journey
analytics
30% more
than their peers

At the same time, all this information about customers, traditionally the domain of data scientists and other left-brained talent, is now being utilized in collaboration with people in creative roles, such as content producers and experience designers. Moving advanced consumer insights out of the background and onto the dynamic front lines of customer engagement gives analysts a new voice within the creative process. They participate in the process of making their work come to life—a new campaign created, an email test sent to a new customer segment, a new on-site or in-store experience deployed. This fosters a sense of empowerment among analysts and helps uncover ideas that would otherwise never see the light of day.

2. They make integration a way of life through an agile marketing operating model.

Integrators have set up structures that allow them to innovate more effectively. At a higher rate than their peers, they have embraced agile marketing and have created small, nimble, cross-functional, colocated, and relatively autonomous teams that execute on single, laser-focused business objectives. Staffed with talent from throughout the marketing department and other areas of the organization, such as IT and operations, these agile teams (or "squads") enable people with different skills sets and backgrounds to sit side-by-side and collaborate with each other on a daily basis. This model brings several marketing functions into a single high-performing team that provides the IT and operations resources needed to bring new ideas to market. In addition, there are typically resources from legal and finance on call to support quick decision making.

This daily and tangible integration bears fruit in three important ways. First, data experts are part of the front-line marketing team. Second, integrated agile teams are able to do more faster. The absence of bottlenecks such as inter-departmental approvals enables frequent and rapid testing of new ideas, content, messages, and value propositions. As a result, the process of creating new campaigns or marketing initiatives often shrinks from months to weeks or even days. Over the last 12 months, integrators in our study were twice as successful as isolators at significantly increasing their speed to market for campaigns or marketing experiments and four times more successful than the idlers.

Finally, there is a quicker and more seamless implementation of technology solutions, thanks to a closer collaboration between marketing and IT (Exhibit 3). Half of the integrators in our study say that marketing and IT work together on a shared vision, versus 22 percent of isolators and 4 percent of idlers. Integrators also use A/B testing 68 percent more often than their peers and are 83 percent more likely to have adopted dynamic creative optimization, a technology that enables modular and dynamic personalized ads and content based on data about the individual consumer. At the other end of the spectrum, 52 percent of companies with the lowest rates of growth admit that their CMO and CTO rarely interact. This lack of coordination takes a toll on the entire marketing organization's ability to deliver omnichannel customer experiences and to track and measure performance in proliferating channels.

Exhibit 3

Integrators are 2x more likely to have Marketing / IT collaboration.

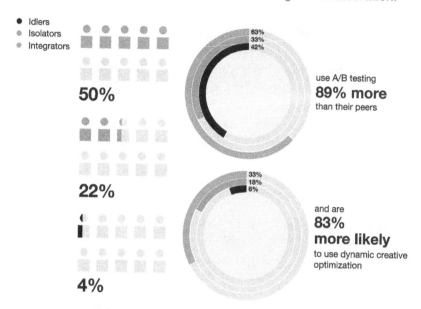

● Idlers
◉ Isolators
◉ Integrators

63%
33%
42%

50%

use A/B testing
89% more
than their peers

22%

33%
18%
6%

and are
**83%
more likely**
to use dynamic creative
optimization

4%

3. They seek "whole-brain" talent.

Hiring an award-winning creative director or a top-flight data scientist used to be enough to up the ante in a marketing department's ability to improve performance. Integrators are now looking for something different. They want talented people who have both left- and right-brain skills, even though their primary function will utilize one more than the other. "There's a misconception that our engineers are not creative and are just 'numbers guys'," the CMO of a leading tech company said. "Actually, they keep us on our toes because they're so creative.

They have extraordinary imagination and turn code into extraordinary products." Additionally, integrators are focused on finding and nurturing people nimble enough to work with colleagues who have different skills and mind-sets than they do.

To ensure that this valuable talent pool has full control over its work product, integrators are increasingly bringing certain marketing functions in-house, particularly those closest to the customer experience, such as consumer insights and data analytics. And because rapid experimentation and testing and learning with new campaigns and designs is so critical, they are insourcing more digital media and content-creation roles. Integrators are the least likely of the three groups we've defined to have one large, full-service ad agency, preferring to use one or more boutique firms that specialize in emerging channels such as augmented and virtual reality, or such innovative capabilities as voice-activated commerce (Exhibit 4).

Exhibit 4

Integrators are 50% more likely to use a variety of agencies for different types of work than their peers.

● Numerous agencies   ● Split creative, media, and digital   ● Predominantly one creative and one media   ● One full-service agency   No agencies

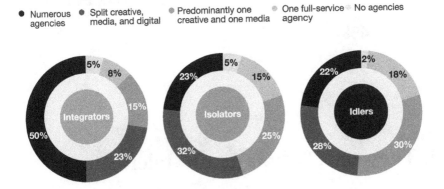

Even these leading marketing organizations don't often achieve their ideals for the recruitment and nurturing of top talent—most say that their talent is somewhere between "on par with our competitors" and "better than competitors but not best in class." Yet they have a

clear understanding of the types of people they want, and they aim high to get them (Exhibit 5).

Exhibit 5

Integrators have better talent across the board though very few best-in-class.
Average score (out of 5)

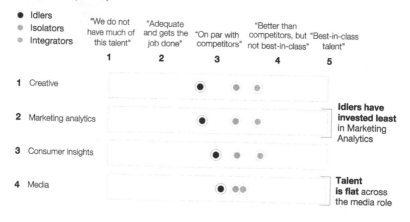

- Idlers
- Isolators
- Integrators

	"We do not have much of this talent" 1	"Adequate and gets the job done" 2	"On par with competitors" 3	"Better than competitors, but not best-in-class" 4	"Best-in-class talent" 5
1 Creative					
2 Marketing analytics					
3 Consumer insights					
4 Media					

Idlers have invested least in Marketing Analytics

Talent is flat across the media role

Room for improvement

Although the integrators in our study excel in data-driven customer experiences, creative use of consumer insights, implementation of agile working models, and collaboration between marketing and technology staff, virtually no companies in our survey stood out across all of the capabilities needed to maximize creativity. There are several for which most companies have much room for improvement, particularly in the area of talent acquisition (Exhibit 6):

Exhibit 6

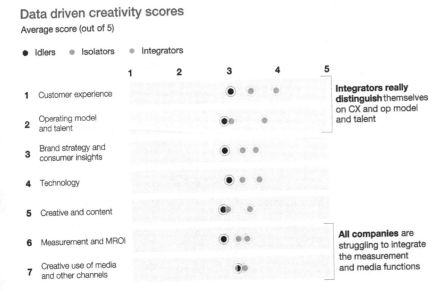

Data driven creativity scores
Average score (out of 5)

● Idlers　　◐ Isolators　　◌ Integrators

		1	2	3	4	5	
1	Customer experience						**Integrators really distinguish** themselves on CX and op model and talent
2	Operating model and talent						
3	Brand strategy and consumer insights						
4	Technology						
5	Creative and content						
6	Measurement and MROI						**All companies** are struggling to integrate the measurement and media functions
7	Creative use of media and other channels						

Measurement

Most companies can track the impact of specific marketing components in direct-response channels such as email and search-engine marketing but struggle to holistically measure channels (both online and offline) *and* attribute the success of a campaign to individual creative, content, and messages. Addressing this challenge requires a "mash-up" of existing technologies and approaches like media-mix modeling, which tracks both online and offline marketing channels; multitouch attribution, which allows companies to track the addressable touchpoints across a customer's journey; and advanced machine learning, which helps combine the two and use adaptive modeling to forecast the impact of shifts in marketing spending. At the moment, very few companies are doing any of this. Even among integrators, only 33 percent say they have the ability to track the ROI of their creative content for all campaigns and in all channels (versus 15 percent of their peers).

AI-driven consumer insights

Artificial intelligence (when thoughtfully applied to protect consumer privacy) can help marketers learn things even the most creative humans can't. By using natural-language processing, for instance, companies can figure out that a consumer is interested in sports cars without the person ever having said so. Computer vision can analyze the videos and images people engage with and infer relevant themes and interests. This deeper understanding of consumer interests, motivations, and attitudes can help develop new value propositions, campaigns and experiences and can drive a pipeline for new products, product extensions, and ecosystem plays that wouldn't be obvious otherwise. Yet despite this potential, only 25 percent of integrators are employing it, versus 10 percent of isolators (Exhibit 7).

Exhibit 7

Integrators use AI 58% more, but only 25% of Integrators are using AI.

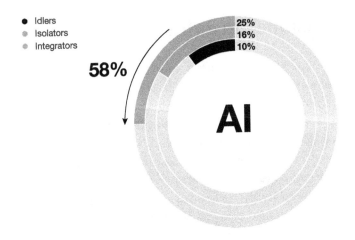

- Idlers
- Isolators
- Integrators

25%
16%
10%

58%

AI

New and creative use of media

All the marketers we surveyed and interviewed, integrators included, felt they were not being creative enough in using media channels, whether dynamic video ads based on content a viewer has watched, mobile video, addressable TV advertising, digital billboards, or custom content integrations with big traditional media players. Aware of the need to engage with their audiences in new ways, traditional media companies have created new ad formats and invested in branded content studios that use their storytelling capabilities to help marketers create more immersive brand experiences.

And despite years of lip service to the need for digital-first content, a majority of companies are still repurposing content and campaigns from traditional channels. This represents a missed opportunity for mobile-tailored ad experiences, heightened consumer engagement with the content, and personalized experiences across all addressable channels.

One CMO in our survey said, "You don't create exciting things for people by figuring out things from data." Actually, we believe that's exactly what data can do. At the end of the day, analytics are what companies have learned about people's behavior. Such insights can guide and inform where imagination needs to go. In the best cases, they can even inspire. Marketers that are leading the pack in driving growth understand that data and human ingenuity are two sides of the same coin.

Strategy to beat the odds

If you internalize the real odds of strategy, you can tame its social side and make big moves.

Several times a year, top management teams enter the strategy room with lofty goals and the best of intentions: they hope to assess their situation and prospects honestly, and mount a decisive, coordinated response toward a common ambition.

Then reality intrudes. By the time they get to the strategy room, they find it is already crowded with egos and competing agendas. Jobs—even careers—are on the line, so caution reigns. The budget process intervenes, too. You may be discussing a five-year strategy, but everyone knows that what really matters is the first-year budget. So, many managers try to secure resources for the coming year while deferring other tough choices as far as possible into the future. One outcome of these dynamics is the hockey-stick projection, confidently showing future success after the all-too-familiar dip in next year's budget. If we had to choose an emblem for strategic planning, this would be it.

In our book, *Strategy Beyond the Hockey Stick* (Wiley, February 2018), we set out to help companies unlock the big moves needed to beat the odds. Another strategy framework? No, we already have plenty of those. Rather, we need to address the real problem: the "social side of strategy," arising from corporate politics, individual incentives, and human biases. How? With evidence. We examined publicly available information on dozens of variables for thousands of companies and found a manageable number of levers that explain more than 80 percent of the up-drift and down-drift in corporate performance. That data can help you assess your strategy's odds of success before you leave the strategy room, much less start to execute the plan.

Such an assessment stands in stark contrast to the norms prevailing in most strategy rooms, where discussion focuses on comparisons with last year, on immediate competitors, and on expectations for the year ahead. There is also precious little room for uncertainty, for exploration of the world beyond the experience of the people in the room, or for bold strategies embracing big moves that can deliver a strong performance jolt. The result? Incremental improvements that leave companies merely playing along with the rest of their industries.

Common as that outcome is, it isn't a necessary one. If you understand the social side of strategy, the odds of strategy revealed by our research, and the power of making big moves, you will dramatically increase your chances of success.

The social side of strategy

Nobel laureate Daniel Kahneman described in his book *Thinking, Fast and Slow* the "inside view" that often emerges when we focus only on the case at hand. This view leads people to extrapolate from their own experiences and data, even when they are attempting something they've never done before. The inside view also is vulnerable to contamination by overconfidence and other cognitive biases, as well as by internal politics.

It's well known by now that people are prone to a wide range of biases such as anchoring, loss aversion, confirmation bias, and attribution error. While these unintentional mental shortcuts help us filter information in our daily lives, they distort the outcomes when we are forced to make big, consequential decisions infrequently and under high uncertainty—exactly the types of decisions we confront in the strategy room. When you bring together people with shared experiences and goals, they wind up telling themselves stories, generally favorable ones. A study found, for instance, that 80 percent of executives believe their product stands out against the competition—but only 8 percent of customers agree.

Then, add agency problems, and the strategy process creates a veritable petri dish for all sorts of dysfunctions to grow.   Presenters seeking to get that all-important "yes" to their plans may define market share so it excludes geographies or segments where their business units are weak, or attribute weak performance to one-off events such as weather, restructuring efforts, or a regulatory change. Executives argue for a large resource allotment in the full knowledge that they will get negotiated down to half of that. Egos, careers, bonuses, and status in the organization all depend to a large extent on how convincingly people present their strategies and the prospects of their business.

That's why people often "sandbag" to avoid risky moves and make triple sure they can hit their targets. Or they play the short game, focusing on performance in the next couple of years in the knowledge that they likely won't be running their division afterward. Emblematic of these strategy-room dynamics is the hockey-stick presentation. Hockey sticks recur with alarming frequency, as the experience of a multinational company, whose disguised results appear in Exhibit 1, demonstrates. The company planned for a breakout in 2011, only to achieve flat results. Undeterred, the team drew another hockey stick for 2012, then 2013, then 2014, then 2015, even as actual results stayed roughly flat, then trailed off.

Exhibit 1

One thing leads to another: Social dynamics and cognitive biases can lead to successive hockey sticks.

EBITDA,[1] disguised example, $ billion

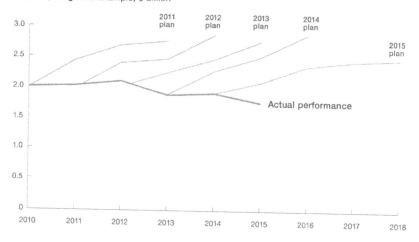

To move beyond hockey sticks and the social forces that cause them, the CEO and the board need an objective, external benchmark.

The odds of strategy

The starting point for developing such a benchmark is embracing the fact that business strategy, at its heart, is about beating the market; that is, defying the power of "perfect" markets to push economic surplus to zero. Economic profit—the total profit after the cost of capital is subtracted—measures the success of that defiance by showing what is left after the forces of competition have played out. From 2010 to 2014, the average company in our database of the world's 2,393 largest corporations reported $920 million in annual operating profit. To make this profit, they used $9,300 million of invested capital, which earned a return of 9.9 percent. After investors and lenders took 8 percent to compensate for use of their funds, that left $180 million in economic profit.

Plotting each company's average economic profit demonstrates a power law—the tails of the curve rise and fall at exponential rates, with long flatlands in the middle (Exhibit 2). The power curve reveals a number of important insights:

Exhibit 2

The power curve of economic profit: The global distribution of economic profit is radically uneven.

Average annual economic profit (EP) generated per company, 2010–14, $ million, n = 2,393[1]

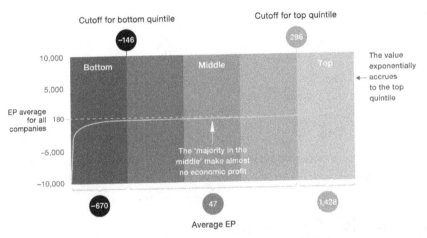

¹Excluding 7 outliers (companies with economic profit above $10 billion or below –$10 billion).

- *Market forces are pretty efficient.* The average company in our sample generates returns that exceed the cost of capital by almost two percentage points, but the market is chipping away at those profits. That brutal competition is why you struggle just to stay in place. For companies in the middle of the power curve, the market takes a heavy toll. Companies in those three quintiles delivered economic profits averaging just $47 million a year.

- *The curve is extremely steep at the bookends.* Companies in the top quintile capture nearly 90 percent of the economic profit created, averaging $1.4 billion annually. In fact, those in the top quintile average some 30 times as much economic profit as those in the middle three quintiles, while the bottom 20 percent suffer deep economic losses. That unevenness exists within the top quintile, too. The top 2 percent together earn about as much as the next 8 percent combined. At the other end of the curve, the undersea canyon of negative economic profit is deep—though not quite as deep as the mountain is high.

- *The curve is getting steeper.* Back in 2000–04, companies in the top quintile captured a collective $186 billion in economic profit. Fast forward a decade and the top quintile earned $684 billion. A similar pattern emerges in the bottom quintile. Since investors seek out companies that offer market-beating returns, capital tends to flow to the top, no matter the geographic or industry boundaries. Companies that started in the top quintile ten years earlier soaked up 50 cents of every dollar of new capital in the decade up to 2014.

- *Size isn't everything, but it isn't nothing, either.* Economic profit reflects the strength of a strategy based not only on the power of its economic formula (measured by the spread of its returns over its cost of capital) but also on how scalable that formula is (measured by how much invested capital it could deploy). Compare Walmart, with a moderate 12 percent return on capital but a whopping $136 billion of invested capital, with Starbucks, which has a huge 50 percent return on capital but is limited by being in a much less scalable category, deploying only $2.6 billion of invested capital. They both generated enormous value, but the difference in economic profit is substantial: $5.3 billion for Walmart versus $1.1 billion for Starbucks.

- *Industry matters, a lot.* Our analysis shows that about 50 percent of your position on the curve is driven by your industry—highlighting just how critical the "where to play" choice is in strategy. Industry performance also follows a power curve, with the same hanging tail and high leading peak. There are 12 tobacco companies in our research, and 9 are in the top quintile. Yet there are 20 paper companies, and none is in the top quintile. The role of industry in a company's position on the power curve is so substantial that it's better to be an average company in a great industry than a great company in an average industry.

- *Mobility is possible—but rare.* Here is a number that's worth mulling: the odds of a company moving from the middle quintiles of the power curve to the top quintile over a ten-year period are 8 percent (Exhibit 3). That means just 1 in 12 companies makes such a leap. These odds are sobering, but they also encourage you to set a high bar: Is your strategy better than the 92 percent of other strategies?

Exhibit 3

What are the odds? Companies have an 8 percent chance of jumping from the middle to the top.

% of companies staying in or moving out of middle 3 quintiles, n = 1,435

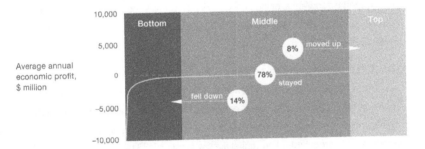

The power of big moves

So what can you do to improve the odds that your company will move up the power curve? The answer is lurking in our data. Consider this analogy: To estimate a person's income, we can start with the global average, or about $15,000 per year. If we know that the person is American, our estimate jumps to the average US per capita income, or $56,000. If we know that the individual is a 55-year-old male, the estimate jumps to $64,500. If that guy works in the IT industry, it jumps to $86,000. And if we know the person is Bill Gates, well, it's a lot more than that.

"...The third little pig wanted to build a wolf-proof brick house. But the other two pigs thought that would take away resources from their budgets, so they talked him out of it right before the wolf killed all three of them."

Adding ever more information similarly helps to zero in on the probabilities of corporate success. Even if you know your overall odds, you need to understand which of your attributes and actions can best help you raise them. We identified ten performance levers and, importantly, how strongly you have to pull them to make a real difference in your strategy's success. We divided these levers into three categories: endowment, trends, and moves. Your endowment is what you start with, and the variables that matter most are your revenue (size), debt level (leverage), and past investment in R&D (innovation). Trends are the winds that are pushing you along, hitting you in the face, or buffeting you from the side. The key variables there are your industry trend and your exposure to growth geographies. In analyzing the odds of moving on the power curve, we found that endowment determines about 30 percent and trends another 25 percent.

The moves that matter

However, it is your moves—what you do with your endowment and how you respond to trends —that make the biggest difference. Our research found that the following five moves, pursued persistently, can get you to where you want to go:

- *Programmatic M&A.* You need a steady stream of deals every year, each amounting to no more than 30 percent of your market cap but adding over ten years to at least 30 percent of your market cap. Corning, which over the course of a decade moved from the bottom to the top quintile of the power curve, shows the value of disciplined M&A. Corning understands that doing three deals a year means it must maintain a steady pipeline of potential targets, conduct due diligence on 20 companies, and submit about five bids.

- *Dynamic reallocation of resources.* Winning companies reallocate capital expenditures at a healthy clip, feeding the units that could produce a major move up the power curve while starving those unlikely to surge. The threshold here is reallocating at least 50 percent of capital expenditure among business units over a decade. When Frans van Houten became Philips' CEO in 2011, the company began divesting itself of legacy assets, including its TV and audio businesses. After this portfolio restructuring, Philips succeeded at reinvigorating its growth engine by reallocating resources to more promising businesses (oral care and healthcare were two priorities) and geographies. Philips started, for example, managing performance and resource allocations at the level of more than 340 business-market combinations, such as power toothbrushes in China and respiratory care in Germany. That led to an acceleration of growth, with the consumer business moving from the company's worst-performing segment to its best-performing one within five years.

- *Strong capital expenditure.* You meet the bar on this lever if you are among the top 20 percent in your industry in your ratio of capital spending to sales. That typically means spending 1.7 times the industry median. Taiwanese semiconductor manufacturer Taiwan Semiconductor Manufacturing Company (TSMC) pulled this lever when the Internet bubble burst and demand for semiconductors dropped sharply. The company bought mission-critical equipment at the trough and was ready to meet the demand as soon as it came back. TSMC had been in a head-to-head race before the downturn but pulled clear of the competition after it ended because of its investment strategy. That laid the foundation for TSMC to become one of the largest and most successful semiconductor manufacturing pure plays in the world.

- *Strength of productivity program.* This means improving productivity at a rate sufficient to put you at least in the top 30 percent of your industry. Global toy and entertainment company Hasbro successfully achieved the top quintile of the power curve with a big move in productivity. Following a series of performance shortfalls, Hasbro consolidated business units and locations, invested in automated processing and customer self-service, reduced head count, and exited loss-making business units. The company's selling, general, and administrative expenses as a proportion of sales fell from an average of 42 percent to 29 percent within ten years. Sales productivity lifted, too—by a lot. Over the decade, Hasbro shed more than a quarter of its workforce yet still grew revenue by 33 percent.

- *Improvements in differentiation.* For business-model innovation and pricing advantages to raise your chances of moving up the power curve, your gross margin needs to reach the top 30 percent in your industry. German broadcaster ProSieben moved to the top quintile of the power curve by shifting its model for a new era of media. For example, it expanded its addressable client base by using a "media for equity" offering for customers whose business would significantly benefit from mass media but who couldn't afford to pay with cash. Some of ProSieben's innovations were costly, sometimes even cannibalizing existing businesses. But, believing the industry would move anyway, the company decided that experimenting with change was a matter of survival first and profitability second. ProSieben's gross margin expanded from 16 percent to 53 percent during our research period.

Greater than the sum of the parts

Big moves are most effective when done in combination—and the worse your endowment or trends, the more moves you need to make. For companies in the middle quintiles, pulling one or two of the five levers more than doubles their odds of rising into the top quintile, from 8 percent to 17 percent. Three big moves boost these odds to 47 percent.

To understand the cumulative power of big moves, consider the experience of Precision Castparts Corp. (PCC). In 2004, the manufacturer of complex metal components and products for the aerospace, power, and industrial markets was lumbering along. Its endowment was unimpressive, with revenues and debt levels in the middle of the pack, and the company had not invested heavily in R&D. PCC's geographic exposure was also limited, though the aerospace industry experienced enormous tailwinds over the following ten years, which helped a lot.

Most important, however, PCC made big moves that collectively shifted its odds of reaching the top quintile significantly. The company did so by surpassing the high-performance thresholds on four of the five levers. For mergers, acquisitions, and divestments, it combined a high value and large volume of deals between 2004 and 2014 through a deliberate and regular program of transactions in the aerospace and power markets.

PCC also reallocated 61 percent of its capital spending among its three major divisions, while managing the rare double feat of both productivity and margin improvements—the only aerospace and defense company in our sample to do so. While nearly doubling its labor productivity, PCC managed to reduce its overhead ratio by three percentage points. It lifted its gross profit-to-sales ratio from 27 to 35 percent.

The combination of a positive industry trend and successful execution of multiple moves makes PCC a showcase of a "high odds" strategy and perhaps explains why Berkshire Hathaway agreed in 2015 to buy PCC for $37.2 billion. Could our model have predicted this outcome? Based on the moves PCC made, its odds of rising to the top were 76 percent.

Patterns of movement

You should be mindful of several dynamics when undertaking major strategic moves. First, our research shows that really big moves can "cancel out" the impact of a poor inheritance. Making strong moves with a poor inheritance is about as valuable as making poor moves with a strong inheritance. And even small improvements in odds have a dramatic impact on the expected payoff, owing to the extremely steep rise of the power curve. For example, the probability-weighted expected value of a middle-tier company increasing its odds to 27 percent from the average of 8 percent is $123 million—nearly three times the total average economic profit for midtier companies.

Big moves are also nonlinear, meaning that just pulling a lever does not help; you need to pull it hard enough to make a difference. For instance, productivity improvements that are roughly in line with the improvement rates of your industry won't provide an upward boost. Even if you are improving on all five measures, what matters is how you stack up against your competitors.

And four of the five big moves are asymmetric. In other words, the upside opportunity far outweighs the downside risk. While M&A is often touted as high risk, for example, in reality programmatic M&A not only increases your odds of moving up the curve but simultaneously decreases your odds of sliding down. Capital expenditures is the one exception. By increasing capital expenditures, your chances of going up on the power curve increase, but so do the chances of dropping.

In general, making no bold moves is probably the most dangerous strategy of all. You not only risk stagnation on the power curve but also miss out on the additional reward of growth capital, which mostly flows to the winners.

So how do you set up a strategy process that embraces a data-based outside view in order to tame the social side of strategy and generate winning, big moves? As we show in our book, there are several practical shifts you can make to transform what happens in your strategy room, such as changing the annual strategy-planning exercise into a continual strategy journey, replacing base-case scenarios with momentum cases that extend the past trajectory into the future, and making strong bets on a few breakout opportunities rather than spreading resources across your divisions.

Adjustments such as these, combined with an empirical, objective benchmark for the quality of a strategy that is independent from subjective judgments in the strategy room, will change the conversation at the top of your company. When you know, ahead of time, the chances of your strategy succeeding, and you can see the levers that matter most to your own business, you can make better choices and mitigate the impact of fear, ambition, rivalry, and bias. A good strategy is still hard to shape, but you can at least navigate toward one based on an accurate map.

The value premium of organic growth

Beware of letting acquisitions take priority over organic growth.

I t's not surprising that many executives think about growth primarily in terms of acquisitions. For some, opportunities to grow organically are limited, especially in maturing or contracting product markets. Others are drawn to the allure of high-profile deal making, with its virtually instant boost to revenues and often earnings per share as well.

But executives shouldn't underestimate the power of organic growth. It may take more time and effort to affect a company's size, but organic growth typically generates more value. A look at the share-price performance of 550 US and European companies over 15 years reveals that for all levels of revenue growth, those with more organic growth generated higher shareholder returns than those whose growth relied more heavily on acquisitions (exhibit). The main reason is that companies don't have to invest as much up front for organic growth.

In growing through acquisition, companies typically have to pay for the stand-alone value of an acquired business plus a takeover premium. This results in a lower return on invested capital compared with growing organically.

At comparable total growth levels, companies with more organic growth outperform those with more growth from acquisitions.

Annualized excess shareholder returns relative to the S&P 500[1]
1999–2013, %

Least organic   Most organic

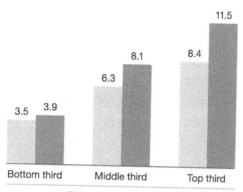

Bottom third   Middle third   Top third

Total revenue growth, %

[1]Excludes banks, insurance companies, extraction companies, and cyclical commodities.

We often see companies pass up organic-growth opportunities because they take longer to boost earnings than acquisitions do. But, given an option, they should probably tip the balance toward what they can achieve organically.

Piloting a biotech leader to greater growth

Growth in a dynamic biotechnology industry requires empowering teams, making real-time adjustments, and shifting the mind-set to accelerate toward the end goal.

A **combination** of thoughtful acquisitions and deliberate leadership has fueled significant and sustained growth for biotech leader Sanofi Genzyme, the specialty-care unit of Sanofi. Bill Sibold, executive vice president and head of Sanofi Genzyme, discusses with McKinsey's Barr Seitz how he has navigated the dynamic biotech marketplace to create that growth.

How do you get the best out of your teams?

Empowerment is critical. If your teams have to run every move up to senior management in a dynamic launch, you've severely hindered yourself. So the goal is to always tell the teams, "You're the experts. You're closest to the data. We want you to act on it." Part of that, though, is senior management's involvement to reinforce that message and also for them to be aware of what's going on in a more fundamental way than just looking at a dashboard report. I attend meetings where we are reading out the launch metrics with the team, so if they have any challenges that they need help with, I can take action on their behalf very quickly or reinforce what they need to do. But my time is limited, so they have to be doing it on their own. But we try to touch base frequently enough so that there is an advocate there to help them get done what they need to get done.

How do you plan a new product launch to support growth?

In any product launch, if you think you know what's going to happen in advance and stick to that plan, I think you're destined for failure. The market's just too dynamic right now. You can't know everything beforehand, and we've taken a lot of pride in making real-time adjustments to our planning based upon the metrics. Now, that is not to say that you just chase the flavor of the day. You need to have the discipline to stick with the core components of the plan while maintaining the flexibility to adjust. For instance, we've had launches where we saw that some of our conversion rates from prescription to patient fulfillment were slower than we had anticipated. So you begin to dissect and do the diagnostic to understand where the patient is falling through the cracks. You can put very specific, targeted plans in place to try to change that component and affect the ultimate metric.

How do you grow in a dynamic market?

Even if you're first-in-class, the time between one launch and the next launch has shrunk so much over time that it just really forces you to move much faster. I think we've seen that in each of our therapeutic areas. You can't afford to have a monthly meeting when you're talking about a dynamic market; you have to meet on a weekly and sometimes daily basis, listening to what you're learning from the market and making adjustments quickly. If you're launching, you have to focus on that. If you have a competitor launching into your space, you need to understand what they're doing and how you might pivot and change your reaction to the competitive pressure. We put extremely high surveillance on each of those areas. When we have a launch, we conduct a daily cross-functional meeting that [considers] all the learnings from the field, from internal, from across our whole service offering, to be able to react to things that we're learning. When a new company is launching in our space, it's the same type of idea: What do we hear they're doing that we can rapidly try in order to get ahead? You just don't have the luxury of spacing things out anymore, and it becomes very much a real-time proposition.

How do you shift thinking about what is possible?

I try to talk in terms of what the big goal is, years down the road when we end a product, in order to get people thinking about accelerating toward that end goal rather than making incremental changes. So if we're launching a product we believe could be something truly extraordinary, the challenge to the team is, "This is where we are going to end up, and it feels like many years away. You have to think about how to really, really, really condense that time. I don't care about your forecast for the quarter or for the year; it's irrelevant. Your eye should be on how to get to that final destination and that condensing of time."

Unleashing the power of small, independent teams

Small, independent teams are the lifeblood of the agile organization. Top executives can unleash them by driving ambition, removing red tape, and helping managers adjust to the new norms.

What does it take to set loose the independent teams that make agile organizations hum? These teams are the organizational units through which agile, project-based work gets done. The typical agile company has several such teams, most composed of a small number of people who have many or all of the skills the team needs to carry out its mission. (Amazon CEO Jeff Bezos contends that a team is too big when it needs more than two pizza pies for lunch.) This multidisciplinary way of composing teams has implications for nearly every business function. Take IT management. Instead of concentrating technology professionals in a central department, agile companies embed software designers and engineers in independent teams, where they can work continually on high-value projects.

While much depends on the actions of the individual team members, senior executives must thoughtfully create the environment in which teams and their managers can thrive. In a nutshell, senior executives must move the company—and themselves—away from outmoded command-and-control behaviors and structures that are ill-suited to today's rapid digital world. They must redouble efforts to overcome resource inertia and break down silos, because independent teams can't overcome these bureaucratic challenges on their own. They must direct teams to the best opportunities, arm them with the best people, give them the tools they need to move fast, and oversee their work with a light but consistent touch. These ideas may sound straightforward, but they go overlooked by too many leaders who've grown up in more traditional organizations.

This article explores how senior leaders can unleash their companies' full potential by empowering small teams and supporting their managers, whose roles have been redefined by agile thinking.

How independent teams work

Several years ago, financial regulators in Europe decided to let banks verify customers' identities remotely through digital video chats instead of relying solely on face-to-face appointments at bank branches. When the news reached one established bank, the team in charge of its know-your-customer (KYC) process recognized that the regulatory change could help the bank win new accounts. It quickly sprang into action to create the needed service. The very existence of this KYC team was a credit to the bank's leaders, who had previously put small, independent teams to work—improving the performance of many of the bank's functions by giving them the diverse capabilities needed to address market opportunities like this one. The bank had simultaneously made a series of complementary reforms to remove cumbersome approval, budgeting, and governance processes. Without these institutional refinements, the KYC team's time to market would have been far less competitive.

Critically, senior executives had endowed small, focused groups like the KYC team with the authority and the resources to carry out projects without first seeking corporate approval. When it came to paying for the development of the digital KYC service, the team was spared the trouble of making a formal budget request and enduring a months-long holding period while the corporate planning committee took up the request as part of its regular planning process. Instead, the team drew on a tranche of funding that it had already been given, funding tied to the team's contribution to outcomes such as higher customer-conversion rates.

The bank also loosened or completely unhitched its product teams' dependence on internal support functions. New accommodations in the bank's HR processes, for example, allowed the KYC team to quickly line up outside contractors for help with front- and back-end development, without waiting for those contractors to be vetted. The IT function had streamlined the bank's technology systems and operations, too, building a modern architecture platform to more easily connect new customer-facing services with legacy back-end systems. The bank had also eliminated its traditional waterfall-development process, as well as a no-compromises protocol for testing new products before launch. Previously, a central IT group would have had to integrate the digital KYC service with core systems, a drawn-out process that could have stalled the KYC team for months. But now the KYC team could integrate testing with work flows, roll out new services as soon as they were viable, and make incremental improvements over multiple cycles. Together, these reforms allowed the KYC team to develop the new digital services in a matter of weeks, rather than the months it would have taken before the reorganization.

Senior company executives had an integral place in this process, despite the independence they had accorded teams like KYC. They evaluated progress and allocated resources according to whether teams deliver against well-defined measures of performance. But they only intervened in the team's ongoing work from time to time, and then only to remove roadblocks and provide support. By creating a supportive structure and managing it with a light touch, senior bank executives fostered this kind of innovative spirit in teams all across the institution.

How executives empower independent teams

The challenge for senior executives in an agile organization is clear but difficult: empower small teams with great independence and resources while retaining accountability. As our colleagues have written, an agile organization speeds up decision making by allowing teams that are closer to customers to make day-to-day, small-stakes decisions on their own, and only escalating decisions that could have significant consequences or that can only be made effectively with input and sign-off from multiple parts of the organization. Executives further empower teams by lessening their dependence on support functions such as finance, planning, and human resources. Yet executives still must ensure that teams operate with proper governance, that company resources are aligned in pursuit of strategic priorities, and that midlevel managers get the coaching they need to become better versed in agile ways of working. Our experience helping companies with the transition to agile ways of working suggests emphasizing the following actions:

Unleash independent teams in meaningful areas

We've argued that autonomy is especially beneficial to teams working on processes and capabilities that directly affect the customer experience. When executives begin to give their small teams more independence, they should look first at teams that are responsible for features that matter greatly to customers. This way, executives can demonstrate how independence helps teams generate more value. (Skeptics may challenge this approach on the grounds that a new, untested way of managing teams is too risky to try in significant customer-facing areas. In practice, independent teams create less business risk, because they make incremental changes that can be rolled back with ease if they don't work out.) It's also important that executives choose teams of people who represent different capabilities. When multiple domains of the company take part in independent teams, executives and managers can test the limits of the decision-making authority that these domains extend to teams, and demonstrate that autonomous teams can be trusted to exercise good judgment.

Put strong performers on independent teams, especially at the outset

Executives can be reluctant to place their best-performing employees on independent teams that aren't mission critical, because they would rather keep them engaged in "more important" activities. We hold the opposite view: that independent teams are too important to the company's future for top performers to be deployed elsewhere. Executives whose companies have been through agile transformations say much the same thing. In an interview with McKinsey, Scott Richardson, chief data officer at Fannie Mae, said, "Creating a new team is probably the most important thing managers can do, so make sure you get it right. When we created our initial agile teams, I was personally involved with structuring them and selecting team members. It might sound crazy to get so involved in this level of detail, but it is critical that the early teams become true beacons for success." Choosing high-caliber people not only sets up the teams to be successful but also teaches managers how to build more independent teams. "By the fourth or fifth team," Richardson continued, "my direct reports knew what questions to ask and how to structure a proper team, and they could scale up on their own from that point forward."

Provide teams with a clear view of their customer

At digital-native companies and agile incumbents, an unwavering focus on improving customer experiences provides each independent team, regardless of its area of responsibility, with a consistent understanding of business priorities. Each team's job is simple: to generate small but frequent improvements in the quality of the customer's experience. Executives foster this shared sense of purpose by making sure that every team has a clear, unobstructed view of customers.

In the offices of one international retailer, real-time data on the customer experience is on display almost everywhere you go. Walk through the dining hall: oversized screens on the walls bear the latest conversion rates for each of the company's sales channels. Visit an independent team's workspace: screens are lit up with measures of customer behavior and satisfaction that relate to the team's responsibilities, such as revising the script that call centers follow or tinkering with the layout of the web storefront. At any moment during the workday, a product manager might drop by a team room to see what the team is working on, ask how customers are responding, and offer to help.

So that each independent team can track the customer experience in ways that are relevant to its work, companies might need to loosen their governance of data. A "canonical data model" that standardizes the classification of data across the entire company can cause inadvertent delays because all teams have to agree on changes to the model that are required to capture new kinds of data or reclassify existing data. To avoid these complications, independent teams are ideally allowed to work with and define data within their business context.

Allocate resources up front, then hold teams accountable

At most companies, teams that work on customer-facing products and services will almost always find a way to obtain the approvals, funds, information, and staff they need for new projects. Scarcity isn't the main problem—slowness is. To eliminate delays in the work of independent teams, executives should assign them all the resources they need to do their work up front: the authority to make key decisions, the ability to quickly hire new talent or secure contractors without going through standard human-resources or procurement processes, the money to cover operating expenses, and so on. These resources should include tools for building and launching whatever digital solutions might be needed to streamline customer journeys or business processes. This kind of self-service approach to application development also requires modular, lightly connected IT architectures, which allow companies to continually develop new applications in a flexible way—an approach one might call "perpetual evolution."

The less dependent on other stakeholders small teams are, the more quickly they can get things done. And since teams invariably encounter unforeseen obstacles, such as a blanket policy preventing them from using public-cloud services, executives have to be there to help. Executives who sponsor the independent teams and make time to hear about their progress and understand their difficulties can push for additional reforms that will keep all independent teams on the fast track.

Once executives have given independent teams more resources and more authority, they need to make sure that those teams are consistently advancing the business's broader strategic priorities. As we'll discuss below, one role for managers in an agile organization is to help independent teams choose the outcomes they will pursue and measure their achievements in precise, meaningful terms. It's the job of top executives to hold teams accountable for delivering those outcomes—and to quickly allocate resources away from disappointing endeavors and toward successful ones. McKinsey research has found that tying budgets to strategic plans is more closely correlated with higher growth and profitability than any other budget-allocation practice that is linked to superior performance.

How executives can empower the agile manager

If the company's squads are going to operate at maximum speed, midlevel managers must learn and practice behaviors that let those units operate in a genuinely agile manner. (See the companion article, "The agile manager.") But if these managers are going to encourage and enable team members, they themselves have to be become well versed, and comfortable, with agility. This won't be an easy task for managers accustomed to the more predictable set of tasks they performed in a command-and-control hierarchy. Senior executives must ensure that these managers learn and embrace new ways of interacting with teams. Here are three behaviors that executives should try to encourage in managers working with small teams:

Define outcomes, then let teams chart their own path toward them

Corporate leaders at agile companies put teams in charge of product features or components of their customer's journey and give them the freedom to decide the specific improvements that should be made. An effective manager in this context will determine what the business outcomes should be, based on the company's overall priorities, and will spell it out for the team using real-world measures of business performance such as conversion rates or audience engagement. Then, rather than dictating the steps a team should take toward those outcomes, the manager must allow the team to chart its own process, intervening only when the team discovers a problem or a need that it can't address on its own.

One retailer greatly increased the pace at which it enhances customer-facing services by giving more authority to a group of small, independent teams. The retailer made the desired business outcome crystal clear: improve conversion rates by 30 percent. But the specifics of how to make that happen were left to the teams. One team responsible for the company's email campaigns decided to test whether targeting smaller groups of customers with highly specialized product offers and sales announcements would lead to more conversions. The team decided to run a trial of the new campaign against a traditional one, and the results were good. That was all the proof it needed to adopt the new approach. No formal proposals or budget discussions or senior-management approvals were required—in fact, any of those steps could have slowed down or derailed the process altogether.

Step inside independent teams to enable their success

Independent teams typically hold a daily "stand-up" meeting of around 20 minutes to review their activities, plans, and difficulties. Then they spend most of their day on productive tasks, rather than administrative ones such as writing formal progress updates.

This manner of working can require major adjustments from managers. They may find their skills in areas like planning and decision making are less needed, while other capabilities, such as communication and problem solving, must be exercised more frequently. Not every manager will welcome the pressure to adapt. Some might start updating their résumés.

Top leaders should encourage these cautious managers to step inside their independent teams. They should join the daily stand-up meetings to hear what the team is doing or try to troubleshoot situations in real time over agile-friendly platforms such as Jira and Slack. Most managers who actively engage in this way come to appreciate the agile approach. An agile organization largely relieves managers of tasks like allocating staff and resources and mapping out projects. Instead, it can spend more time on higher-value activities: applying expertise to long-term matters, coaching team members and peers, and helping teams work around obstacles.

A top-performing software developer at a rather traditional company that was still engaged in the waterfall style of software development passed up several promotions that would have put him in charge of development teams. He preferred grappling with technical challenges and writing code to managing people. But after the company reorganized its customer-facing functions into independent teams, his prospects changed considerably. He continues to work as a developer, but he also leads a network of coaches who teach the company's independent teams to follow agile ways of working. The new job combines technical assignments with the responsibility to share his expertise in agile development—and has none of the traditional management tasks that he had long avoided.

Commit to retraining managers for their redefined roles

Outside the IT function, managers who understand agile ways of working can be hard to find at traditional companies. To fit in with highly independent teams, most managers will need some help to learn how to organize their thinking around products rather than processes; to direct teams with performance goals instead of work plans; and to position themselves as stewards, not superiors. Executives can, and should, make sure that their managers have opportunities to develop these behaviors and habits of mind. They can see that managers are taught to use new tools, from collaboration software to analytics engines. They can encourage managers to rotate through assignments with various independent teams, which promotes constant learning. They should pair them with fellow managers who have more experience working with independent teams and let them see how these peers behave. And they can change the way they evaluate managers' performance, placing more emphasis on measurable outcomes and gauging their impact through 360-degree reviews.

Alfred Chandler, the renowned business historian, famously observed that structure follows strategy: companies set their strategies, then organize themselves in a way that lets them carry out their strategies to full effect. But pressure from fast-moving digital natives and digitally transformed incumbents means that traditional businesses no longer have time to rethink their strategies and reorganize themselves every few years. To promote enterprise agility, more companies are choosing to make small teams their basic organizational unit. Problems occur, however, when companies don't give their small teams enough autonomy to work at the speed required by the digital economy. Executives can change this by giving the teams the resources they need, by eliminating red tape, and by encouraging managers to learn, adopt, and enact the more flexible governance methods of agile organizational approaches. Those who do will see their small teams become more independent, and more capable of producing innovations and performance gains that keep their businesses ahead of the competition.

Choosing the right path to growth

To boost organic growth, most companies need a diverse set of initiatives —and how you sequence them matters.

Innovation and growth are often lumped together as management concepts, for good reason: it's self-evident that innovation drives growth, and conspicuous fast growers often benefit from high-profile innovations. Our research, however, suggests growth-minded companies stand to benefit by disaggregating the two concepts. There are, in fact, multiple paths to growth, and the most common growth characteristics among above-average growers often aren't related to innovation. Significant as well, companies aspiring to the highest levels of growth need to sequence their initiatives carefully. Put differently: you probably can't do everything at once.

How many levers?

In earlier research, we explored three broad profiles that describe how companies achieve organic growth. "Investors" tap new sources of funding or reallocate existing funds to capture new growth for their goods and services. "Creators" build business value with new products or through business-model innovation. "Performers" grow by steadily optimizing commercial functions and operations. Our latest findings suggest that focusing on two of these growth levers simultaneously will spur growth more effectively than emphasizing one.

In fact, we found that more than three-quarters of companies that mastered two or more levers grew faster than their industry (Exhibit 1). This makes intuitive sense; combining two approaches allows for synergies that can multiply impact. Companies with strong reallocation practices (investors), for example, can provide managers with the needed additional resources to optimize higher-potential assets (performers). Too often, this sort of helpful one-two punch is the exception: companies instead tend to emphasize what worked in the past, and thus to rely too heavily on a single lens—which leaves potential growth on the table.

Exhibit 1

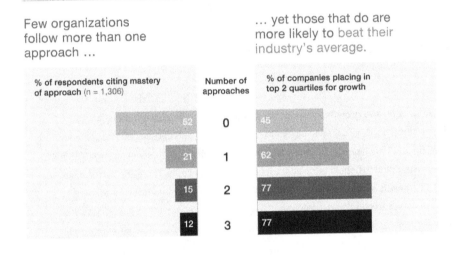

Few organizations follow more than one approach ...

... yet those that do are more likely to beat their industry's average.

% of respondents citing mastery of approach (n = 1,306)

Number of approaches

% of companies placing in top 2 quartiles for growth

% of respondents citing mastery of approach (n = 1,306)	Number of approaches	% of companies placing in top 2 quartiles for growth
52	0	45
21	1	62
15	2	77
12	3	77

What about three levers? In some sense, it's the gold standard; a healthy proportion of top-growth-quartile companies were investors, performers, and creators.[3] That said, executing on every front simultaneously is more than many companies can handle. That's particularly the case for large organizations, where complexity tends to multiply as growth initiatives proliferate.

The power and limitations of innovation-led growth

Exhibit 2

Innovative companies that have mastered creative capabilities are more heavily represented among the fastest growers.

Companies' likelihood to have mastered a lens compared with those in a lower quartile, %

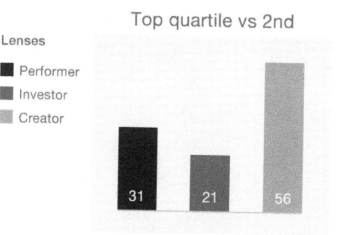

Top quartile vs 2nd

Lenses
- ■ Performer
- ■ Investor
- ■ Creator

31 21 56

Creative companies are more heavily represented among the fastest growers. And the ability to innovate consistently appears to separate the *good* growers in the second quartile from *exceptional* ones in the top quartile. We found that exceptional growers were 56 percent more likely to have mastered creative practices (that is, reached the 70 percent successful adoption level) than the second-quartile firms (Exhibit 2).

What's also true, however, is that it's hard to get innovation right: nearly half of all the companies surveyed were weakest in creative practices, while fewer than one in five said innovation was an area of greatest strength. In addition, our research suggests that the pursuit of innovation is not the surest way to move into the top-growth tiers. Rather, the most prevalent practices among above-average growers reflected mastery of core *investor* and *performer* levers (Exhibit 3). Three of the top five practices characterizing upper-tier growers were related to investing: aligning on priority markets, engaging in portfolio management informed by prospective returns, and overseeing resources top down. Two more were tied to performing: developing high-value customer development across business units and measuring the voice of customers. The prevalence among high performers of strengths related to smart resource allocation and strong commercial performance suggests that they are more than mere table stakes for growth and that executives should not take them for granted, even if they seem rudimentary.

Exhibit 3

Third-quartile companies emphasized performance, while those in
the second quartile worked equally on performance and investment.

Companies' likelihood to have mastered a lens
compared with those in a lower quartile, %

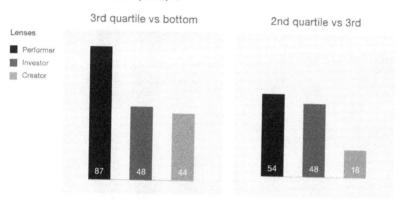

Lenses
■ Performer
■ Investor
▨ Creator

3rd quartile vs bottom   2nd quartile vs 3rd

87 48 44   54 48 18

Sequencing the growth journey

Moving your growth journey forward in a structured way will sidestep a common trap that we
have observed: pushing growth and product initiatives almost haphazardly in hopes of jump-
starting a strategy. Instead, companies need a more deliberate, stepwise approach to building
growth initiatives and capabilities. While there is no iron law of sequencing, the data are clear
that a steady pace of change is vital: we found a positive correlation between the number of
growth best practices adopted by a company and the company's growth-performance
quartile (Exhibit 4). Across all companies surveyed, we found that employing two additional
practices, on average, correlated with an organic-growth edge ranging from one to three
percentage points. Companies that regularly fine-tune and add to their capabilities appear to
improve their odds of generating steady performance gains, providing additional resources
that leaders can reallocate, as needed, to further their growth agenda.

Exhibit 4

Higher rates of best-practice adoption are correlated with higher growth-performance quartiles.

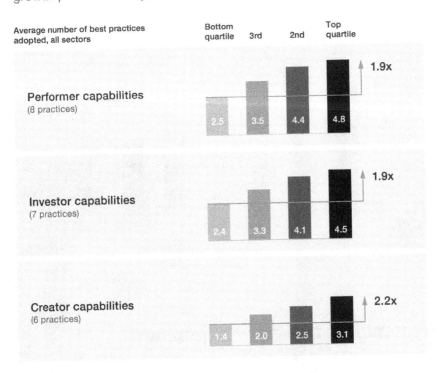

Average number of best practices adopted, all sectors

	Bottom quartile	3rd	2nd	Top quartile

Performer capabilities
(8 practices)

2.5 · 3.5 · 4.4 · 4.8 — 1.9x

Investor capabilities
(7 practices)

2.4 · 3.3 · 4.1 · 4.5 — 1.9x

Creator capabilities
(6 practices)

1.4 · 2.0 · 2.5 · 3.1 — 2.2x

Getting this right, in our experience, goes hand in hand with rigorous initiative and performance management, which includes rallying organizational support for growth priorities; supporting them with capability building, incentives, and cultural change; and looking for opportunities to exploit synergies among new business initiatives. That's the path a global manufacturer is following as it strives to shift its growth performance in critical markets from lagging to leading. The company has started by upgrading the effectiveness of its transactional pricing, marketing tactics, and core sales force—priorities that, leaders believe, will help it hold its own against rivals. Looking forward, the senior team is studying more ambitious initiatives to accelerate growth, surpass competitors, and increase market share. One avenue, for example, would boost the use of advanced data analytics, to gather deeper insights on customer-procurement practices and emerging product preferences. Those data and greater mobilization across functions would help managers uncover and share insights about untapped growth opportunities. Margin improvements from the initial steps would provide the means, confidence, and capabilities for more innovative efforts. Sales teams, R&D, and product-development functions, for example, would be able use the data-driven knowledge about customers and markets to collaborate more closely on new, higher-margin offerings aimed at nascent customer preferences.

Growth is difficult, but our research shows that it's possible to bring a disciplined approach to improving your growth trajectory. Build momentum through well-sequenced initiatives. Support them with the right capabilities. And get your organization on board with a multifaceted approach that often will rest on a strong foundation of resource allocation and execution before taking on the tougher discipline of innovation. While this may challenge some traditional growth tenets, it also offers a reason to start moving—with confidence. What you do well today prepares the way for the next leg of the climb.

The importance of a growth-leadership mind-set in capturing growth

Business leaders need three capabilities to drive growth: mind-set, curiosity, and a willingness to adapt to the client and the market.

In this interview, McKinsey's Biljana Cvetanovski talks to Capita Chief Growth Officer Ismail Amla about the growth-leadership mind-set. Capita is an international outsourcing company headquartered in London, with revenues of £3.9 billion. The following is an edited version of the interview.

How do you think about a growth leadership mind-set?

When I was growing up, my dad used to tell me, "If you think you're going to do it, you're going to be right. If you think you're not going to do it, you're going to be right." A growth-leadership mind-set, for me, is the neuroscience confirming the hypothesis that how you think determines how you feel and how you behave, and how you behave determines the outcome. So in the growth-leadership mind-set we have the ability to try, fail, and learn from that. We have the ability to move at a pace that we've not moved at before. We have the ability to overcome obstacles. It gets you to a place where you're thinking about how you make things happen, rather than how they can't be changed.

From the growth perspective, the growth-leadership mind-set is really critical. As I describe it to my team, it's one of the three mandatory non-negotiables. If you're not in a growth-leadership mind-set, you really can't be playing a leadership role in growth. We can evidence it by how people behave, how they act, how they collaborate, what they take to clients, how they deal with failure. All of those things actually lead to how we show up in front of clients.

What are the core capabilities required to drive growth?

I think the first one is around curiosity. This has been termed in the market as "consultative selling," which is how you get to a place where you can really understand what the client wants. The second that I think is really important is learning agility. What we're finding is it's not as important to know something as it is to be able to learn something. What our clients are going through, especially in years of disruption, is usually that they are not experts and we are collaborating with them as we're learning what their problems are and how we may be able to solve them. Then the third thing is the ability to have the growth mind-set.

What is the role of a growth leader?

My remit is to support the businesses to be relevant to our clients tomorrow and in the future. What that means is really professionalizing the sales and marketing capability. Secondly, it's around playing the transformation role, because growing and aligning with our clients generally means that the full value chain in our business needs to change. So the way the developer works, the way the account manager works and relates to our clients, the way we do service delivery, all play a huge part in whether we can grow. So the second role is actually creating a transformation activity which allows us to be able to change to be able to support our growth.

Then the third thing is to be able to look over the horizon and see, for example, that the markets and our clients are being disrupted in a certain way, so we need to disrupt ourselves. As a chief growth officer, I would hold myself accountable whether we grew and when, whether it's this quarter, the next half year, or the year after.

The 90% success recipe: How digital and analytics can help commercial transformations beat the odds and the market

Pressure is mounting on CEOs and business leaders to deliver above-market growth. Consistently beating the market over time, however, requires a top-performing commercial engine underpinned by a new wave of digital and analytics capabilities.

While hiring new talent is a crucial component of building necessary capabilities, our experience has shown that developing a market-beating company requires change that comes within the organization itself. Business executives today need to focus on building capabilities with the same level of commitment they showed when transforming their businesses through lean operations in the 1980s.

That prospect, however, is daunting considering that, traditionally, less than a third of transformations have succeeded as expected. A staggering 70 percent of the failures are due to an organization's inability to adopt required new behaviors quickly and completely. At the same time, leaders often doom any transformation effort by being overly tentative about changing their commercial structures for fear of disrupting sales activities. This level of change requires significant courage and leadership.

A new approach to commercial transformation (embedding digital, analytical, and agile skills into marketing, sales, and pricing capabilities to drive revenues and/or margin improvements) is turning that failure rate on its head. We have found an astonishing 90 percent of companies that embrace this new approach to overhauling their commercial drivers are not only delivering above-market growth but also sustaining it over time. Furthermore, two-thirds of all companies pushing these transformations are achieving this in either profitability or revenue growth, and a quarter are achieving it in both.

The case for change

While most major companies understand the need to adapt to the marketplace, we find that they often don't have the level of commitment needed for a commercial transformation to succeed over time. Increasingly, however, the decision for change is one that leadership can't put off. Better commercial capabilities are necessary to respond to something that we observe more and more often in the marketplace: Competitive advantage just doesn't last very long anymore. Competitors spot and adapt to innovations and new products quickly, and that reality is just going to accelerate as companies build out more digital and analytical capabilities.

"Sometimes we'll spend a lot of time bringing a product to market, and we need to plan for the fact that that gives us only a six-month head start," says Gary Booker, CMO for Dixons Retail. "We need to then figure out, whilst our competitors are catching up with what we've just done, what we're doing to make sure that when they get there we're already on to the next thing."

What that means in practice is having an agile organization that is constantly innovating, constantly spotting and reacting to new opportunities. It is a business that is constantly improving its understanding of how, what, and when the customer wants to interact and buy.

Erwin van Laethem, CEO for Dutch energy company Essent, puts is succinctly: "Every success we've had in the market has been copied by our competitors. What you can't copy is how people work together in an organization."

Our research demonstrates that companies with more advanced marketing and sales capabilities tend to grow their revenue 30 percent more than the average company within their sector. (See exhibit). What's more, those companies with leading digital capabilities, are growing 5× faster than their peers.

Furthermore, successful commercial transformations have delivered consistently impressive results: A chemicals company grew revenue 7 percent annually while cutting marketing and sales costs by 8 percent; a manufacturer saw a 3-5 percent uptick in revenue based on revised marketing plans; a paper and packaging company is on track to increase ROIC from 6 percent to 10 percent in three years, thanks to its program to build a continuous-improvement mindset in marketing and sales.

The case for change is clear; how to do it is less so. How have these commercial transformations succeeded where others before have faltered? Our experience leading 100 commercial transformations in the past five years, together with the results from a survey of 2,300 executives and our Digital Quotient ™ database, distilled the recipe for success into the following six components:

1. Know where you are and where you're going

"You need to create the compelling case for change. Define what problem the organization is trying to solve and why the current status is not good enough." That's the advice of one European chief commercial officer, and it crystallizes where any transformation should start. A clear vision is essential and should be based on insights from data rather than on hunches.

Typically, companies don't have a strong sense of their commercial capabilities. High-performing companies, however, systematically assess their capabilities at a granular enough level to allow executives to take meaningful action. The best companies are deliberate about identifying their strengths and weaknesses against all capabilities and then mapping them against their goals so they understand which capabilities to prioritize. Everyone in the C-suite must be able to articulate what two to three commercial capabilities their organization is focused on building, how they are building them, and how well the capability-building effort is translating into impact. High performing companies have been focusing particularly on their digital capabilities across marketing, sales, and IT strategy, culture, and organization.

Leading companies use intense multiday workshops to distill this initial vision into concrete targets and timelines that can be filtered down from the leadership team. Connecting a visionary goal with a clear and pragmatic timeline creates tremendous energy to start the transformation.

2. Create a transformation team built on trust

With the aspirations and fact base in place, the next stage is to create a resilient commercial-transformation team. While it is typically led by either the CEO, head of sales, CMO, or sometimes even the COO, it should include marketing, sales, operations, data analytics/scientists, and business-unit leaders. Team members need to be respected—their day-to-day colleagues should feel they can't afford to lose them. It is also important to include HR and communications professionals alongside a project manager who keeps everyone focused on the next step of the journey and tracks the relevant metrics.

Since commercial transformations are long processes and involve taking risks, the team must invest time in building deep levels of trust to keep morale high over time. We've found that 63 percent of successful commercial transformations balance team health with performance. Activities to build that trust should focus on learning what really makes each person tick, understanding motivations, and identifying attitudes towards change and risk.

To kick start team building at a healthcare company, for instance, executives went on an offsite that included an extreme ropes course and an outdoor orienteering exercise where some team members were blindfolded. Trust builds quickly when you're dangling 50 feet above the ground or relying on someone else to see. The second half of the offsite focused on sharing stories, often personal ones related to issues that employees might not otherwise bring up in the workplace but that can explain behaviors with a major impact on a transformation.

What matters is that the team members understand their own motivations and those of their colleagues as they embark on a transformational journey that definitely involves new experiences and risks.

3. Score quick wins

Transformations will not succeed unless they deliver substantive short-term wins within six to twelve months. Typically, therefore, the best companies build momentum by focusing first on initiatives that have early impact—and help fund the transformation—then on building a case for further change efforts.

A heavy-equipment manufacturer discovered there was a large consumer market of people who liked the brand but couldn't easily buy the products because they were sold only through B2B sales channels. As a result, the company quickly moved its mid-priced product line into big-box retailers, thus gaining access to the consumer segment. Revenues grew by 10 percent within just eight months.

Aside from the additional revenue, this success proved that the company could get its products into new segments through both targeted marketing and building relationships with retailers, without upsetting its traditional sellers. In the longer term, this quick win moved customer insights to the heart of everything the company did and proved to any skeptics that the transformation into a customer-solutions organization was both worth pursuing and achievable.

To help accelerate the process, many companies are also embracing, at least in parts of their organization, the notion of agile. This capability boils down to having a dedicated approach to constantly testing, learning, and evolving ideas and solutions based on getting quick results and clear data-driven insights.

4. Activate the organization

Working with leadership, the transformation team has to structure a plan for pushing change throughout the organization. That requires a clear vision for building new habits at every level of the organization. For the C-suite, it's about mindset change and developing new leadership and change-management skills. For managers, the focus needs to be on coaching, product knowledge, and problem solving. Frontline reps need specific selling skills like consultative selling and using pricing analytics. You can't do everything at once, of course, so the team needs to carefully sequence the effort, from rolling out training sessions to doing field work to reinforcing habits through e-learning, for example.

Activating an entire organization also requires finding the right people to make the change happen throughout the business. More than 60 percent of our survey respondents said that having committed change leaders across the organization was "extremely important" to the transformation effort. At a packaging company, senior managers used network-analysis and organizational-health-index tools to discover who would be "up for the battle," in the words of one marketing director. The company ran a survey to identify to whom staff turned when they had questions, and who was trusted. The results revealed the most influential people at key points across the organization, and they were invited to become "change champions." These are the people who have to reinforce the messages relentlessly and deliver the change on the ground.

Imaginative communications are also necessary so that everyone continues to sit up, take notice, and act. These may involve internal or even external advertising campaigns, social media, town hall meetings, and a raft of other communication efforts.

5. Commit to coaching

Coaching is so critical for success that we want to highlight it specifically. Good coaching is much more than going on a ride-along with your buddies or doing a sales pitch while someone watches. It's about a real commitment to improving your people by providing constructive feedback, empathizing, helping them work through issues, and reinforcing their strengths ... at the right cadence. It's also about role modeling new behaviors, something that rarely happens in practice.

The CEO of a business division said that "personal development through manager coaching is now a hallmark of how we run our business." It's clear that success doesn't just come from shiny new tools; it comes from breaking old habits. But turning sales managers into coaches requires a change in behavior. One company provided managers with training in traditional skills such as handling difficult conversations and assigned a "supercoach" to each sales manager. These coaches, drawn from its central sales-training team, observed real-life coaching interactions between managers and sales reps and gave specific feedback on the managers' coaching skills. The company credits the enhanced coaching role of the sales managers with a resulting 25 percent improvement in close rates.

In sales, companies have found that a structured coaching program with at least weekly contact between coach and sales rep is vital to changing how people work. For example, a consumer-services company mandates that sales managers conduct daily 15-minute check-in calls with all reps who fail to hit their monthly targets. Reps who make their targets get weekly one-on-one sessions, and reps who exceed their targets get a 10-minute praise call every week. The company also requires managers to join each rep for a day every month.

Such regular and frequent team touchpoints can be vital to the success of pilot projects. One company held weekly meetings at which the team could plot strategy for the week ahead. The results of the first pilots exceeded all aspirations. Sales calls per rep rose by 40 percent, offers closed per sales team rocketed by 75 percent, and the average contract value per week rose by 80 percent—and by as much as 150 percent for new deals. These results were achieved with the same sales reps and managers who had previously been underperforming. It was the company's approach to performance management rather than the specific tools that made the difference.

6. Hardwire a performance culture

The reality of today's economy is that change is constant. Hard-wiring a high-performance culture into a company's DNA is the only way to assure growth above the market year after year.

As Tom O'Brien, group vice president and general manager, marketing & sales, at Sasol, says of the pricing transformation he led: "The real success of this is not if we deliver two to three billion, but if we deliver that and then identify another two to three billion, and deliver on that, again and again."

Building this culture requires putting in place specific processes and tools to redirect the organization, reinforce behavior, and build new habits. But the really critical component is putting in place the right metrics to track and adjust performance. Without them, it's virtually impossible to understand what is and isn't working.

The best-performing companies develop dashboards to track progress. They include basic financial-performance metrics, of course, but importantly they also track indicators of changes in behavior, such as understanding how marketing is helping the salesforce sell, which tools helped close sales, and how often collaboration meetings occurred.

These companies also actively track capability metrics, such as training courses their people have taken, whether they passed or failed, and how that correlates with performance in the field. They then use those calculations to adjust their capability-building efforts and zero in on weak performers who need more or different training.

The companies that effect a successful transformation go one step further by adding surveys and in-person interviews with their people to provide an even more comprehensive picture of commercial performance. They also develop customer-satisfaction measures—using sales, business units, and pricing as the "customers" of marketing. To be most effective, measurement must start before a transformation kicks in, in order to create a baseline. Then at regular intervals, companies measure again to understand what progress has been made at both the organizational and capability levels.

One multinational industrial company took this comprehensive commercial view of metrics and discovered a big gap between what sales reps were doing in the field and what their distributors actually wanted from them. Although the product and pricing were good, their distributors wanted to visualize the product and calculate the cost and payoff of various product options. They found further that the things marketing was creating, such as brochures, weren't helping with the sales process. Sales decided to ask marketing to create a calculator that would help tabulate the answers to distributor questions in real time.

As a European marketing director put it, "The organization needs to be—and stay—hungry. Focus on what needs to be done, and then ensure you sustain it."

While metrics are important to track performance (e.g. traffic, conversion, transaction size, etc), they also need to support a performance culture. Commercial leaders put in place metrics to measure test and learn progress and agile A/B testing approaches, for example.

116

These metrics can help avoid paralysis by analysis by helping employees track their performance in a way that encourages learning as you go to drive progress, incremental improvements, and quick feedback loops with your customers.

A new breed of commercial transformation is rewriting the playbook on how to deliver successful, sustained, above-market growth. At least as much investment is needed in organizational culture and health as in the intricacies of what will change on the ground. This makes transformation challenging, yes, but it also means the rewards are substantial.

Not only do all the pieces of the transformational jigsaw have to fit, but the picture they create has to be clear and easily understood by everyone. A strong leader needs to ensure that the enthusiasm, energy and momentum is sustained throughout the process. It's likely to be one of the most challenging things a company undertakes—but it has the potential to be the most rewarding both for your people and for achieving above-market growth.

Taking the measure of innovation

Don't overlook the insight that two simple metrics can yield about the effectiveness of your R&D spending.

You've probably heard the old joke about the two economists who saw $20 on the sidewalk. "Look," exclaimed the first economist, "a $20 bill!" "It can't be," the other economist answered. "If it were a $20 bill, someone would have already picked it up."

We were reminded of this story when we began to notice a pair of innovation metrics that seemed so intuitive that we assumed they must have been conspicuously applied and rejected before. So far, however, we've found no indication of widespread use—and a reasonable amount of evidence suggesting that, at least for most industries, the measurements work.

We call these indicators R&D conversion metrics: R&D-to-product (RDP) conversion and new-products-to-margin (NPM) conversion. Their core components—gross margin, R&D, and sales from new products—are not new, but combining them can reveal fresh insight on the relative innovation performance of business units, within an organization and relative to external peers (Exhibit 1). The first metric, RDP, is computed by taking the ratio of R&D spend (as a percentage of sales) to sales from new products. This allows organizations to track the efficacy with which R&D dollars translate into new-product sales. The second metric, NPM, takes the ratio of gross margin percentage to sales from new products, which provides an indication of the contribution that new-product sales make to margin uplift.

Exhibit 1

Two metrics combine R&D spending, sales from new products, and gross margin to shed light on relative innovation performance.

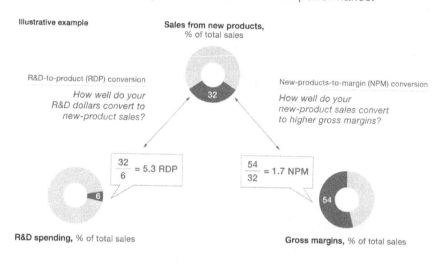

Illustrative example

Sales from new products, % of total sales

R&D-to-product (RDP) conversion

How well do your R&D dollars convert to new-product sales?

New-products-to-margin (NPM) conversion

How well do your new-product sales convert to higher gross margins?

$$\frac{32}{6} = 5.3 \text{ RDP}$$

$$\frac{54}{32} = 1.7 \text{ NPM}$$

R&D spending, % of total sales

Gross margins, % of total sales

Notably, these metrics can be gauged outside in, making them ideal for benchmarking. They also apply on the portfolio level, where the net effect of individual project investments reflects the results as a whole. That broader perspective accords with how senior executives and investors typically consider innovation performance. It's not the most granular way to consider project value creation, and it doesn't aspire to be. In seeking the ideal metric, one should not let the perfect be the enemy of the good. When a business can convert a high rate of R&D dollars to new products, and when its new products flow through to higher gross margins, good things will happen.

As we'd expect, the R&D conversion metrics show that higher spend does not inevitably translate to stronger performance. That should come as no surprise to seasoned executives and analysts. Rather, when we benchmarked companies within select industries, results varied markedly. The R&D conversion metrics also demonstrate—sometimes strikingly— where some organizations are falling short and where opportunities for improvement may be found (Exhibit 2). Not every company that scores strongly on RDP is able to follow through to higher margins, and a company scoring above-median performance on NPM may underperform in RDP.

Exhibit 2

Taken together, the R&D conversion metrics can help identify favorable and unfavorable innovation-performance outliers.

New-products-to-margin (NPM) conversion,
gross margin per $ of new-product sales

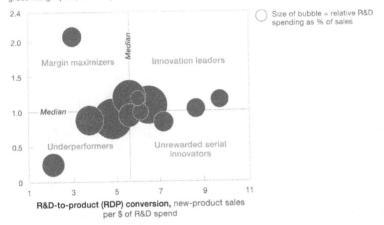

Source: Capital IQ; company investor presentations

While the R&D conversion metrics are useful, context is essential. Benchmarking must be conducted against comparable firms—pure plays versus pure plays, diversified companies against companies with multiple business lines, and product-to-product comparisons with cycle times that are as close in duration as possible. These metrics also work best in industries where product turnover is higher and the incremental effect of innovation is both more immediate and more critical to the business model. For example, in specialty chemicals and consumer goods, two industries with rapid innovation cycles, the three-year average in gross margins correlates strongly with the five-year average of new-product sales. In industries with markedly longer cycles, such as pharmaceuticals and agribusiness, the r-squareds are lower.

But in a real sense, those exceptions help prove the rule: the more that innovation matters with immediacy, the more insight is to be gained by tracking your innovation efforts. In our experience, many companies spend too much time looking inward at measures of activity (for example, number of patents, or progress of ideas through a pipeline), and not enough scrutinizing the returns on innovation. Creating value is the name of the game, and these R&D conversion metrics help you keep score.

How to modernize an established brand to drive growth

The key to Wendy's successful transformation? Staying true to the brand while using data to better serve customers.

Modernizing a cherished brand without alienating a loyal customer base or losing market share in a hypercompetitive marketplace is challenging. The hurdles include continuing to drive and maintain growth, choosing the right ideas for big results, knowing the customer, and innovating while staying true to the brand's roots. Kurt Kane, chief concept and marketing officer at Wendy's, spoke with McKinsey partner Stacey Haas and discussed how the restaurant chain tackled these challenges.

The ingredients for sustained growth

We're now at 22 consecutive quarters of same-restaurant sales growth. And honestly, it's due to a very simple formula that Dave Thomas put in place when he founded the chain back in 1969: put quality first, and be very specific with customers about the differences between Wendy's and our competitors. Also, treat people with respect, and do the right thing.

Deciding how to drive growth

Some of our toughest debates about choices for driving growth often come down to which products to launch and what we can execute successfully in our restaurants.

There's always a natural tension in the restaurant business between marketing and restaurant operations, because marketers are really good at creating fun ideas. But sometimes a new idea can put unfair stress on the restaurant without generating a big enough return to warrant the effort that goes into it. You have to make sure everybody's grounded and everything you do is built around improving the economic model.

Modernizing the brand's tone of voice

What I found is that our customers love the Wendy's brand but have wanted us to modernize it for a long time. They've been rooting for the brand, love our food, and were hanging in there with us, even though the brand had gotten a little dated and tired.

So for us, the challenge was to bring those restaurants back to life in a very different way.

I think the thing that let us modernize our brand's tone of voice, particularly in social, is that we've stayed grounded in what Dave Thomas did when he first started advertising Wendy's nationally. He was always willing to pick a fight with the competition.

Knowing which ideas to pursue and which to reject

We test a lot of different ideas. Some of them work, some of them don't, and some of them work great. I think the key thing is not doing those that only do okay. Those okay, safe, middle-of-the-road ideas rarely lead to a big result, and you can waste a lot of money, time, and energy very quickly. There's a long list of okay ideas that we've decided not to do, and that's allowed us to pick two or three big ideas and drive those out.

It can be hard to choose not to do something. There have been many times when I or other senior leaders on my team walk into a room and say, "Look, we're not going to do that," even though people have put their hearts and souls into it. That's simply because it didn't get a big enough result. But the work that was done got us to a jumping-off point to go find that bigger idea.

Taking risks

You've got to be willing to get yourself in trouble now and then to get people's attention. Probably my biggest troublemaking moment here at Wendy's was the time we decided to release our own hip-hop album on social media, but we didn't tell our franchise system, and we didn't tell a lot of our key partners. We just decided to push it out. We didn't know it was going to be as big as it turned out to be. But I didn't do a good job of telling people what we were up to and why, because it was an idea that had been initially rejected or at least created a lot of concern. So my biggest troublemaking moment turned out to be a big success.

Turning customer knowledge into profits

Back in 2015, we invented a new promotional concept called "4 for $4," where we gave people a complete meal solution for $4. It transformed the velocity of our business. We attracted a lot of new customers, and they were incredibly appreciative of the value they could get with the high-quality food we were offering.

The way 4 for $4 came about was by listening to customers, who were looking for a complete meal for under $5. So we looked at our menu and realized we could cobble together a great meal, a very filling meal, for under $5 if we cherry-picked the right items from the menu. Instead of forcing consumers to figure that out themselves, we just did it for them, and we immediately saw a massive lift when we bundled it all together.

Using data analytics to unlock creativity

To me, data has always been the way to unlock creativity. We had very specific data around what consumers were able to spend and what we could offer on our menu. We then had to solve that problem, because those two things weren't working well together. We all sat in a room, put our creative minds together, and explored the ways that we could deliver. That's when we invented 4 for $4. Then we had to challenge ourselves to make that concept interesting through advertising and communications.

Data is all about identifying the problem you're trying to solve. Then you bring creativity to deliver solutions. Whenever you're providing solutions for a consumer problem, your business grows.

Balancing spending between channels

We still do a lot of traditional media. We buy a lot of television, and we do that to spread awareness quickly about new initiatives we're bringing to the market. There's still no better way to do that. But television continues to get more expensive, so we're aggressively moving more of our dollars into digital. What I do find, though, is the more disruptive we are with social, the less we have to spend. Because one of our rules on anything that we do in social—and through traditional media—is that we had better get a lot of press out of it.

We have only a quarter of the dollars that our largest competitor has to spend, so we need to make those dollars work extra hard. And we've been very fortunate that we've gotten a lot of media attention out of many of our moves, because we've had the courage to do some disruptive things.

Innovating while staying true to your roots

When you think about all the different food trends that are out there, and how Wendy's can deliver well against those, I think the most important thing is to not chase a trend but stay true to what you do uniquely well.

For us, we did a lot of research. We asked people for all the different things that could motivate them to buy hamburgers, for example, and what they told us was that the most important thing we could do was deliver a hamburger made with fresh—never frozen—beef, hot off the grill.

The new model for consumer goods

Why the industry's historic value-creation model is faltering—and how to reinvent it.

The fast-moving-consumer-goods industry has a long history of generating reliable growth through mass brands. But the model that fueled industry success now faces great pressure as consumer behaviors shift and the channel landscape changes. To win in the coming decades, FMCGs need to reduce their reliance on mass brands and offline mass channels and embrace an agile operating model focused on brand relevance rather than synergies.

A winning model for creating value

For many decades, the FMCG industry has enjoyed undeniable success. By 2010, the industry had created 23 of the world's top 100 brands and had grown total return to shareholders (TRS) almost 15 percent a year for 45 years—performance second only to the materials industry.

The FMCG value-creation model

This success owed much to a widely used five-part model for creating value. Pioneered just after World War II, the model has seen little change since then. FMCG companies did the following:

- *Perfected mass-market brand building and product innovation.* This capability achieved reliable growth and gross margins that are typically 25 percent above nonbranded players.

- *Built relationships with grocers and other mass retailers that provide advantaged access to consumers.* By partnering on innovation and in-store execution and tightly aligning their supply chains, FMCG companies secured broad distribution as their partners grew. Small competitors lacked such access.

- *Entered developing markets early and actively cultivated their categories as consumers became wealthier.* This proved a tremendous source of growth—generating 75 percent of revenue growth in the sector over the past decade.

- *Designed their operating models for consistent execution and cost reduction.* Most have increased centralization in order to continue pushing costs down. This synergy-based model has kept general and administrative expenses at 4 to 6 percent of revenue.

- *Used M&A to consolidate markets and create a basis for organic growth post acquisition.* After updating their portfolios with new brands and categories, these companies applied their superior distribution and business practices to grow those brands and categories.

Signs of stagnating success

But this long-successful model of value creation has lost considerable steam. Performance, especially top-line growth, is slipping in most subsegments. The household-products area, for example, has dropped from the sixth most profit-generating industry at the start of the century to the tenth, measured by economic profit. Food products, long the most challenging FMCG subsegment, fell from 21st place to 32nd. As a consequence, FMCG companies' growth in TRS lagged the S&P 500 by three percentage points from 2012 to 2017. As recently as 2001–08, their TRS growth beat the S&P by 6 percent a year.

The issue is organic growth. From 2012 to 2015, the FMCG industry grew organic revenue at 2.5 percent net of M&A, foreign-exchange effects, and inflation, a figure that is a bit lower than global GDP over the period. But companies with net revenue of more than $8 billion grew at only 1.5 percent (55 percent of GDP), while companies under $2 billion grew at twice the large company rate.

This difference suggests that large companies face a serious growth penalty, which they are not making up for through their minor expansion in earnings before interest and taxes (Exhibit 1).

Exhibit 1

Organic fast-moving-consumer-goods (FMCG) industry growth has been weak, with large companies growing at only 55 percent of GDP.

2012–16 performance of FMCGs larger than $400 million in net revenue

	Reported growth, CAGR,[1] %	Real organic growth (M&A, foreign exchange, and inflation adjusted), CAGR,[1] %	Median EBIT[2] margin expansion, percentage points
All FMCGs (n = 290)	6.0	2.5	0.6
Large, >$8 billion (n = 57)	3.7	1.5	1.1
Medium, $2 billion to $8 billion (n = 102)	6.3	2.6	0.1
Small, $0.4 billion to $2 billion (n = 131)	6.7	3.0	0.6
2012–16 real GDP growth, CAGR[1]		2.7	

55% of GDP

[1] Compound annual growth rate.
[2] Earnings before interest and taxes.

This growth challenge really matters because of the particular importance of organic growth in the consumer-goods industry. FMCG companies that achieve above-market revenue growth and margin expansion generate 1.6 times as much TRS growth as players who only outperform on margin.

Ten disruptive trends that the industry cannot ignore

Why has this FMCG model of value creation stopped generating growth? Because ten technology-driven trends have disrupted the marketplace so much that the model is out of touch. Most of these trends are in their infancy but will have significant impact on the model within the next five years (Exhibit 2).

Exhibit 2

Ten trends are disrupting the historic value-creation model in the fast-moving-consumer-goods (FMCG) industry.

FMCG industry's 5-part model for value creation

Moderate 1 2 3 4 5 Very high

	Value created	10 disruptive trends	Trend impact	
			Past 5 years	Next 5 years
1 Excellence in mass-market product innovation and brand building, including premiumization	• Stable growth • 25% gross margin advantage over nonbranded players	• The millennial effect • Digital intimacy (data, mobile, IoT¹) • Explosion of small brands • Better for you	2 2 2 3	4 5 4 5
2 Advantaged consumer access via mass-trade relationships	• Broad distribution • Limited competitive set	• E-commerce giants • Discounters • Mass-merchant squeeze	2 2	5 5
3 Developing market-category creation alongside rising incomes	• 75% of FMCG revenue growth over past 10 years	• Rise of local competitors	2	3
4 Operating model that drives consistent execution and achieves cost reduction	• ~4–6% general and administrative	• Pressure for profit from activist investors	2	4
5 M&A to consolidate markets and enable organic growth post acquisition	• Attractive market structure • Opportunity to step change organic revenue growth	• Building competition for deals	2	2

¹Internet of Things.

Disruption of mass-market product innovation and brand building

Four of the ten trends threaten the most important element of the current model—mass-market product innovation and brand building.

The millennial effect

Consumers under 35 differ fundamentally from older generations in ways that make mass brands and channels ill suited to them. They tend to prefer new brands, especially in food products. According to recent McKinsey research, millennials are almost four times more likely than baby boomers to avoid buying products from "the big food companies."

And while millennials are obsessed with research, they resist brand-owned marketing and look instead to learn about brands from each other. They also tend to believe that newer brands are better or more innovative, and they prefer not to shop in mass channels. Further, they are much more open to sharing personal information, allowing born-digital challenger brands to target them with more tailored propositions and with greater marketing-spend efficiency.

Millennials are generally willing to pay for special things, including daily food. For everything else, they seek value. Millennials in the United States are 9 percent poorer than Gen Xers were at the same age, so they have much less to spend and choose carefully what to buy and where to buy it.

Digital intimacy (data, mobile, and the Internet of Things [IoT])

Digital is revolutionizing how consumers learn about and engage with brands and how companies learn about and engage with consumers. Yesterday's marketing standards and mass channels are firmly on the path to obsolescence. Digital-device penetration, the IoT, and digital profiles are increasing the volume of data collected year after year, boosting companies' capabilities but also consumer expectations. Most FMCGs have started to embrace digital but have far to go, especially in adopting truly data-driven marketing and sales practices.

Some FMCG categories, particularly homecare, will be revolutionized by the IoT. We will see the IoT convert some product needs, like laundry, into service needs. And in many categories, the IoT will reshape the consumer decision journey, especially by facilitating more automatic replenishment.

Explosion of small brands

Many small consumer-goods companies are capitalizing on millennial preferences and digital marketing to grow very fast. These brands can be hard to spot because they are often sold online or in channels not covered by the syndicated data that the industry has historically relied on heavily.

But venture capitalists have spotted these small companies. More than 4,000 of them have received $9.8 billion of venture funding over the past ten years—$7.2 billion of it in the past four years alone, a major uptick from previous years (Exhibit 3). This funding is fueling the growth of challenger brands in niches across categories.

Exhibit 3

The venture-capital industry is fueling the explosion of small brands, providing $7.2 billion in investment in the past four years alone.

Total venture-capital investment by year, $ million

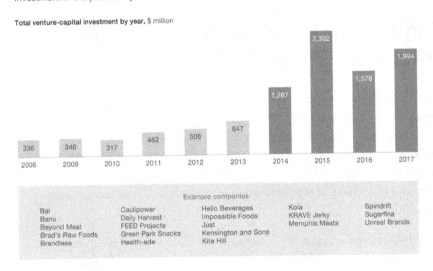

Retailers have also taken notice of these small brands. According to The Nielsen Company, US retailers are giving small brands double their fair share of new listings. The reason is twofold: retailers want small brands to differentiate their proposition and to drive their margins, as these small brands tend to be premium and rarely promote. As a consequence, small brands are capturing two to three times their fair share of growth while the largest brands remain flat or in slight decline (Exhibit 4).

Exhibit 4

Small companies are generating two to three times their fair share of growth in developed markets.

Fast-moving-consumer-goods industry share of sales and of growth, 2016–17

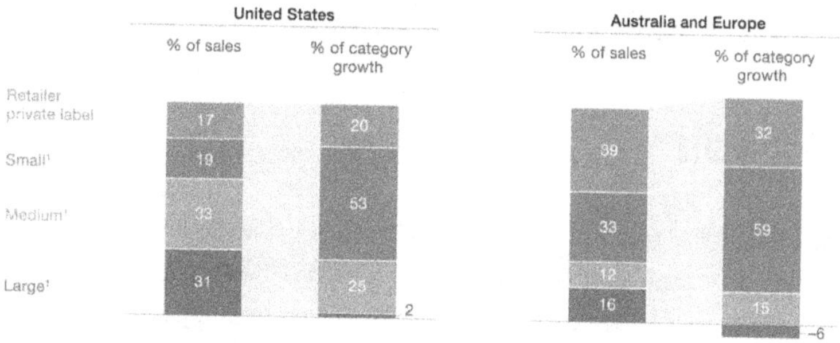

	United States		Australia and Europe	
	% of sales	% of category growth	% of sales	% of category growth
Retailer private label	17	20	89	32
Small¹	19			
Medium¹	33	53	33	59
Large¹	31	25	12	15
		2	16	–6

¹"Large" refers to top 16 companies, "medium" to next 400 companies, and "small" to remaining companies.

Five factors make a category ripe for disruption by small brands. High margins make the category worth pursuing. Strong emotional engagement means consumers notice and appreciate new brands and products. A value chain that is easy to outsource makes it much easier for born-digital players to get started and to scale. Low shipment costs as a percent of product value make the economics work. And low regulatory barriers mean that anyone can get involved. Most consumer-goods categories fit this profile.

The beauty category in particular is an especially good fit, so the advanced explosion of small brands in this category is no surprise. In color cosmetics, born-digital challenger brands already represent 10 percent of the market and are growing four times faster than the rest of the segment. The explosion of small brands in beauty enjoys the support of significant venture-capital investment—$1.6 billion from 2008 to 2017, with 80 percent of this investment since 2014.

At the same time, digital marketing is fueling this challenger-brand growth while lifting the rest of the category, as beauty lovers find new ways to indulge in their passion. An astounding 1.5 million beauty-related videos are posted on YouTube every month, almost all of them user generated.

We believe that this bellwether category portends well for FMCG incumbents. After a few challenging years, the incumbent beauty players are responding effectively and are mobilizing to capitalize on the dynamism in their industry, particularly through greater digital engagement. They are innovating in digital marketing and running successful incubators. The year 2016 alone saw 52 acquisitions of beauty-related companies.

Better for you

For years, consumers said that they wanted to eat healthier foods and live healthier lifestyles, but their behavior did not change—until now. Consumers are eating differently, redefining what healthy means, and demanding more products that are natural, green, organic and/or free from sugar, gluten, pesticides, and other additives. Packaged-food players are racing to keep up, even as consumers are increasing pressure on the packaged-goods subsector by eating more fresh food.

Disruption of mass-retailer relationships

Three trends are fueling a fierce business-model battle in retail. The e-commerce giants are already the clear winners, while the discounter business model is also flourishing. Mass merchants are feeling the squeeze.

E-commerce giants

E-commerce giants Amazon, Alibaba Group, and JD.com grew gross merchandise value at an amazing rate of 34 percent a year from 2012 to 2017. As their offer attracts consumers across categories, they are having a profound impact on consumer decision journeys. This change requires FMCGs to rewrite their channel strategies and their channel-management approaches, including how they assort, price, promote, and merchandise their products, not just in these marketplaces but elsewhere. This disruption is in early days in markets other than China and will accelerate as the e-commerce giants increase their geographic reach and move in to brick-and-mortar locations. Amazon's push on private labels is a further game changer. To see the future, we can look to how China FMCG retailing has been revolutionized by Alibaba Group and JD.com and the profound impact Amazon has had on its early categories like electronics, books, and toys.

Discounters

ALDI and LIDL have grown at 5.5 percent from 2012 to 2017, and they are looking to the US market for growth. Discounters typically grow to secure market share of 20 percent or more in each grocery market they enter. This presence proves the consumer appeal of the format, which enables discounters to price an offering of about 1,000 fast-moving SKUs 20 percent below mass grocers while still generating healthy returns.

Mass-merchant squeeze

The rise of the e-commerce giants and the discounters is squeezing grocers and other omnichannel mass merchants. Together, the seven largest mass players saw flat revenue from 2012 to 2017. This pressure is forcing mass merchants to become tougher trading partners. They are pursuing more aggressive procurement strategies, including participating in buying alliances, getting tighter on SKU proliferation, and decreasing inventory levels. They are also seeking out small brands and strengthening their private labels in their quest for differentiation and traffic.

Disruption of developing-market category creation: The rise of local competitors

Developing markets still have tremendous growth potential. They are likely to generate new consumer sales of $11 trillion by 2025, which is the equivalent of 170 Procter & Gambles.

But local competitors will fight for that business in ways the multinational FMCGs have not seen in the past. As new competitors offer locally relevant products and win local talent, FMCG companies will need to respond—which will challenge the fairly centralized decision-making models that most of them use.

Further, channels in developing markets are evolving differently than they did in the West, which will require FMCGs to update their go-to-market approaches. Discounter-like formats are doing well in many markets, and mobile will obviously continue to play a critical, leapfrogging role.

Disruption of the synergy-focused operating model: Pressure for profit

Driven by activist investors, the market has set higher expectations for spend transparency and redeployment of resources for growth. Large FMCGs are being compelled to implement models such as zero-based budgeting that focus relentlessly on cost reduction. These approaches, in turn, typically reduce spend on activities such as marketing that investors argue do not generate enough value to justify their expense. While this approach is effective at increasing short-term profit, its ability to generate longer-term winning TRS, which requires growth, is unproven.

Disruption of M&A: Increasing competition for deals

M&A will remain an important market-consolidation tool and an important foundation for organic revenue growth in the years following an acquisition. But some sectors like over-the-counter drugs will see greater competition for deals, especially as large assets grow scarce and private-equity firms provide more and more funding.

Of course, the importance of these ten disruptive trends will vary by category. But five of the trends—the millennial effect, digital intimacy, the explosion of small brands, the e-commerce giants, and the mass-merchant squeeze—will deliver strong shocks to all categories (Exhibit 5).

Exhibit 5

The historic value-creation model for fast-moving consumer goods will be affected in several ways.

1	**Excellence in mass-market product innovation and brand building, including premiumization**	• Most category growth will be in niches • The portion of consumers that resist or reject mass brands will increase, especially in food products • Consumers' preferred method of learning about brands will be listening to each other • Small brands will thrive given their easy access to consumers, fit with millennial preferences, and pull from mass merchants seeking to differentiate themselves • New data sources will become more important than syndicated data for understanding the market and managing performance; having an accurate picture will become a competitive advantage • The Internet of Things will convert some product needs to service needs and change the consumer decision journey in many categories
2	**Advantaged consumer access via mass-trade relationships**	• The e-commerce giants will lead the trade • Discounters will grow to ~20% in most markets • Mass merchants will feel the "squeeze" and fight back with greater use of buying alliances, better use of owned data, and keenness for differentiation • Factors will push down pricing, which will require consumer-packaged-goods companies to live within a lower gross-margin structure
3	**Developing-market category creation alongside rising incomes**	• Developing markets will remain a great source of value creation; local players will fight for it • Channel evolution will leapfrog developed markets, especially in mobile
4	**Operating model that drives consistent execution and achieves cost reduction**	• Local relevance, consumer closeness, and speed will become more important than consistent execution as a driver of competitive advantage • Activist investors will continue to promote a cost agenda
5	**M&A to consolidate markets and enable organic growth post acquisition**	• Large assets will become scarce in some categories • Deep pockets of private equity will drive up valuations

---

A new model for creating value in a reshaped marketplace

To survive and thrive in the coming decades, FMCG companies will need a new model for value creation, which will start with a new, three-part portfolio strategy. Today, FMCGs focus most of their energy on large, mass brands. Tomorrow, they will also need to leapfrog in developing markets and hothouse premium niches.

This three-part portfolio strategy will require a new operating model that abandons the historic synergy focus for a truly agile approach that focuses relentlessly on consumer relevance, helps companies build new commercial capabilities, and unlocks the true potential of employee talent. M&A will remain a critical accelerator of growth, not only for access to new growth and scale, but also new skills (Exhibit 6).

Exhibit 6

The new model for fast-moving consumer goods is a three-part portfolio strategy enabled by an agile operating model, with continued use of M&A as an accelerator.

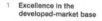

3-part portfolio strategy	1 Excellence in the developed-market base	2 Leapfrogging in developing markets	3 Hothousing premium niches, scaling each to its greatest potential
	Relentless focus on innovation that generates incrementality	Bringing best technologies to market early	Innovation based on rapid test and learn
	Daily excellence in execution, including use of advanced analytics to drive insights, marketing spend, revenue management, production, and supply	Market leadership in digital/mobile	Targeted digital marketing
		Local market autonomy to fight microbattles and ensure local relevance	Full use of channels, including retailer e-commerce and direct to consumer
	Joined-up, channel-conflict-resistant sales approach that wins with omnichannel mass and e-commerce giants		Supply capability adapted to small runs and shipments

Agile operating model	4 Agile organization: dynamic front end, stable backbone

Semiautonomous agile teams				
Digital/IT capability	Data and advanced analytics capability	Mass supply system	Niche supply system	Back-office functions

5 Continued use of M&A as an accelerator to drive market consolidation and fuel organic growth, including programmatic M&A skills, post acquisition

Broader, three-part portfolio strategy

Today, most FMCGs devote most of their energy to mass brands. Going forward, they will need excellence in mass-brand execution as well as the consumer insights, flexibility, and execution capabilities to leapfrog in developing markets and to hothouse premium niches.

Sustaining excellence in the developed-market base

Mass brands in developed markets represent the majority of sales for most FMCGs; as such, they are "too big to fail." FMCGs must keep the base healthy. The good news is that the industry keeps advancing functional excellence, through better technology and, increasingly, use of advanced analytics. The highest-impact advances we see are revamping media spend, particularly through programmatic M&A and understanding of return on investment, fine-tuning revenue growth management with big data and tools like choice models, strengthening demand forecasting, and using robotics to improve shared services.

In addition to taking functional excellence to the next level, FMCGs will need to focus relentlessly on innovation to meet the demands of their core mass and upper-mass markets.

FMCGs will need to increase their pace of testing and innovating and adopt a "now, new, next" approach to ensure that they have a pipeline of sales-stimulating incremental innovation (now), efforts trained on breakthrough innovation (new), and true game changers (next).

Further, FMCGs will need to gather their historically decentralized sales function, adopting a channel-conflict-resistant approach to sales. They will need to treat e-commerce as part of their core business, overcome channel conflict, and maximize their success in omni and e-marketplaces. Players like Koninklijke Philips that have weathered the laborious process of harmonizing trade terms across markets are finding that they can grow profitably on e-marketplaces.

Finally, FMCGs will need to keep driving costs down. We are following three big ideas on cost.

First, zero-based budgeting achieves sustained cost reduction by establishing deep transparency on every cost driver, enabling comparability and fair benchmarking by separating price from quality, and establishing strict cost governance through cost-category owners who are responsible for managing cost categories across business-unit profits and losses.

Second, touchless supply-chain and sales-and-operations planning replace frequent sales-and-operations meetings with a technology-enabled planning process that operates with a high degree of automation and at greater speed than manual processes.

Third, advanced analytics and digital technologies improve manufacturing performance by pulling levers like better predictive maintenance, use of augmented reality to enable remote troubleshooting by experts, and use of advance analytics for real-time optimization of process parameters to increase throughput yield of good-quality product.

Many of these changes will require strengthening technology—making it a core competency, not a cost center.

Leapfrogging new category creation in developing markets

FMCG companies must bring their newest and best innovation, not lower-quality products, into developing markets early to capture a share of the $11 trillion potential growth. Success will require excellent digital execution, as many of these markets will grow up to be digital. Success will also require empowering local leadership to compete with the local players looking to seize the market's growth potential. Local leaders will need decision rights on marketing as well as a route to market that is joined up across traditional, omni, and e-marketplace channels.

Hothousing premium niches

FMCG companies must identify and cultivate premium niches that have attractive economics and high growth potential to capitalize on the explosion of small brands. Success will require acquiring or building small businesses and helping them reach their full potential through a fit-for-purpose commercialization and distribution model. This means, for example, building a supply chain that produces small batches and can adapt as companies learn from consumers. The beauty industry's incubators are a good model here.

The demands of this three-part portfolio strategy call for a new, agile operating model that allows a company to adapt and drive relevance rather than prioritizing synergy and consistent execution above other objectives.

Agile operating model

Originating in software engineering, the concept of an agile operating model has extended successfully into many other industries, most significantly banking. Agile promises to address many of the challenges facing the traditional FMCG synergy-focused model.

Building an agile operating model requires abandoning the traditional command-and-control structure, where direction cascades from leadership to middle management to the front line, in favor of viewing the organization as an organism. This organism consists of a network of teams, all advancing in a single direction, but each given the autonomy to meet their particular goals in the ways that they consider best. In this model, the role of leadership changes from order-giver to enabler ("servant leader"), helping the teams achieve their goals.

An agile operating model has two essential components—the dynamic front end and the stable backbone. Together, they bring the company closer to customers, increase productivity, and improve employee engagement.

The dynamic front end, the defining element of an agile organization, consists of small, cross-functional teams ("squads") that work to meet specific business objectives. The teams manage their own efforts by meeting daily to prioritize work, allocate tasks, and review progress; using regular customer-feedback loops; and coordinating with other teams to accomplish their shared goals.

The stable backbone provides the capabilities that agile teams need to achieve their objectives. The backbone includes clear rights and accountabilities, expertise, efficient core processes, shared values and purpose, and the data and technology needed for a simple, efficient back office.

The agile organization moves fast. Decision and learning cycles are rapid. Work proceeds in short iterations rather than in the traditional, long stage-gate process. Teams use testing and learning to minimize risk and generate constant product enhancements. The agile organization employs next-generation technology to enable collaboration and rapid iteration while reducing cost.

We also expect the FMCG operating model of the future to be more unbundled, relying on external providers to handle various activities, while FMCGs perhaps provide their own services to others.

M&A as an accelerator

M&A will remain critical to FMCG companies as a way to pivot the portfolio toward growth and improve market structure. The strongest FMCGs will develop the skills of serial acquirers adept at acquiring both small and large assets and at using M&A to achieve visionary and strategic goals—redefining categories, building platforms and ecosystems, getting to scale quickly, and accessing technology and data through partnership. These FMCGs will complement their M&A capability with absorbing and scaling capabilities, such as incubators or accelerators for small players, and initiatives to help their teams and functions support and capitalize on the changing business.

Moving forward

To determine how best to respond to the changing marketplace, FMCG companies should take the following three steps:

- *Take stock of your health by category in light of current and future disruption, and decide how fast to act.* This means asking questions about the external market: how significantly are our consumers changing? How well positioned are we to respond to these changes? What are the scale and trajectory of competitors that syndicated data do not track? Is our growth and rate of innovation higher than these competitors, particularly niche competitors? How advanced are competitors on making model changes that might represent competitive disadvantages for us? How healthy are our channel partners' business models, and to what degree are we at risk? Do our future plans take advantage of growth tailwinds and attractive niches? Answering these questions creates the basis for developing scenarios on how rapidly change will happen and how the current business model might fare in each scenario.

- *Draft the old-model-to-new-model changes that will position the company for success over the next decade.* This is the time to develop a three-part portfolio strategy and begin the multiyear transformation needed to become an agile organization, perhaps by launching and then scaling agile pilots. This is also the time to determine which capabilities to prioritize and build and the time to redesign the operating model, applying agile concepts and incorporating the IT capabilities that offer competitive advantage. Change management and talent assessment to determine where hiring or reskilling are needed will be critical.

- *Develop an action plan.* The plan should include an ambitious timeline for making the needed changes and recruiting the talent required to execute the plan.

These efforts should proceed with controlled urgency. Over time, they will wean FMCG companies from reliance on the strategies and capabilities of the traditional model. Of course, as companies proceed down this path, they will need to make ever-greater use of the consumer insights, innovation expertise and speed, and activation capabilities that have led the industry to success and will do so again.

Building an engine for growth that funds itself

You don't have to look far to finance your growth ambitions.

To drive growth, you first have to find the fuel—and for many companies, that's not so straightforward. Internal and external obstacles, including onerous approval processes, and short-term stock-market impact, can make it hard to fund promising ventures. But it doesn't have to be that way.

Our research shows that many companies that consistently post top-line growth operate with what we call an investor mind-set. They continually squeeze funds from underperforming areas and allocate the savings to new ventures or existing programs that have the potential to scale. In other words, they fund their own growth.

As simple as that might sound, this investor approach is a significant departure for many executives, who tend to be consumed with cutting costs and playing it safe by banking marginal gains. They fall victim to a common behavior that drives only short-term profit: taking the savings from often highly disciplined cost-cutting programs and dropping the cash to the bottom line.

Growth leaders are different. They constantly scour for savings across the business. They know exactly where each incremental dollar of savings should be reinvested to drive new growth, and they know the ROI of every dollar invested. In our experience, it often takes a significant event, such as a new CEO or business-unit leader, an acquisition, or a transformation to turn around a declining business, to jolt the business into action. While these catalysts are effective motivators, business leaders intent on driving growth (and in some industries or sectors facing stiff headwinds, investing only in growth might not be the best option) don't have to wait for them to occur to build the Investor DNA into their organization.

This Investor approach is most effective as part of a purposeful and diversified approach to driving growth (Exhibit 1).

Exhibit 1

Three strategies for organic growth

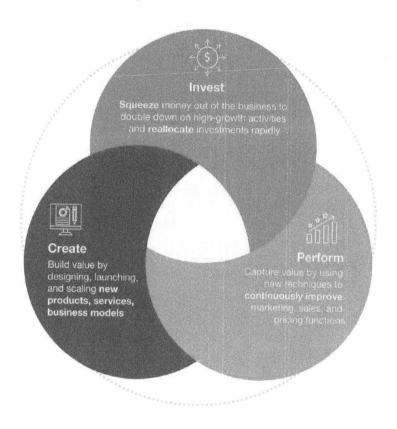

The Performer approach, where businesses continually optimize commercial functions (marketing, sales, and pricing) can yield a massive source of investment funding. The Creator approach pours those investments into new products, services, or business models to drive future growth. The true power of the Investor profile is reflected in a recent McKinsey survey, which revealed that 51 percent of top-growth companies use Invest as their primary growth approach (vs. 20 percent for Create and 28 percent for Perform), though there is significant variance by sector (the Investor premium is significant in pharma, for example, but much less so in automotive and assembly).

How to think and act like an Investor

For companies looking to jump-start their growth ambitions, the Investor approach can be a fast way to achieve results. Investing in proven winners—initiatives that are already driving growth but may be underfunded—can put points on the board quickly. Sustaining that, however, requires leaders to be intentional in making the necessary commitments to change the business's growth trajectory. That includes making a number of "big moves" (as our colleagues who authored *Strategy Beyond the Hockey Stick* call them) to improve productivity and dynamically reallocate funds. It also requires putting in place new processes and using data to make better decisions. In fact, data and analytics are the top differentiating capabilities between high-growth Investor companies and their peers, according to McKinsey research (Exhibit 2).

Exhibit 2

Overview of the Investor approach to funding your growth

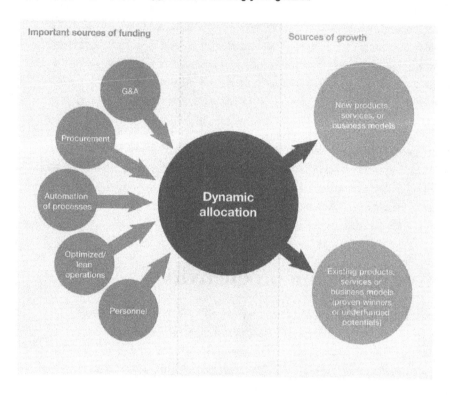

1. Find the money and squeeze

Investor companies can uncover hundreds of millions of dollars in savings. This isn't some theoretical pot of money that will materialize in the distant future; often, companies can begin banking the new funds in a matter of weeks or months. Here are three steps high-performing companies take to find the biggest savings opportunities:

Get real about transparency

For growth leaders, there's no such thing as black-box spending, in which you invest money in a service or program and wait to see how it works out. Instead, these companies insist on radical transparency, demanding to know the exact purpose of each dollar spent as well as the anticipated return. They put in place processes, metrics, and simple dashboards that allow them to get a clearer view of how their spend is performing. Increasingly, we're seeing the maturation of IoT technologies that can now provide near real-time insights into process and performance, particularly in logistics, supply-chain management, and manufacturing.

On the commercial front, Western Union provides an example of a systematic approach to bringing transparency to media activities. The company embarked on a program to break down the efficiency and effectiveness of its media spend. It consolidated its agency roster and improved the way it negotiated commercial terms with its agencies. That work included developing a better understanding of costs, which allowed it to be more precise about bidding out the work. The company also put in place different effectiveness measures.

Drive maximum productivity

Just as underperforming programs sometimes continue to receive funding out of inertia, some processes may continue to churn along even though there are faster, cheaper alternatives. High-performing Investor companies continually scour their organization for outdated, inefficient ways of operating. To get the full benefits of productivity, each process should be in the top 30 percent for the industry. A few of the most promising areas of focus are:

- **Efficiency.** Leading companies engage in detailed process mapping, looking for opportunities to streamline operations, eliminate redundant processes, and hunt down opportunities to rationalize partnerships. Advanced analytics has emerged as a powerful capability in driving new levels of efficiency. Utility transmission and distribution operators, for example, that are able to use advanced analytics to predict maintenance activities can reduce their costs by 10 to 20 percent, while improving asset reliability.   Simplification can also be useful in improving efficiency. One telecom provider reduced its product portfolio by 80 percent before streamlining its digital experience and supporting platform.

- **Procurement.** Adding rigor to procurement of products and services by benchmarking prices, soliciting bids, moving some services in house, and driving for transparency can unlock significant savings. When it comes to marketing, we've found that by analyzing ongoing costs such as agency and overhead, companies can uncover savings of 10 to 20 percent on marketing spend. Digital has the potential to radically increase savings as well. In a recent McKinsey survey, chief procurement officers said they expect their digital procurement programs to increase annual savings by 40 percent.

- **Automation.** Advances in analytics have allowed companies to unlock significant efficiencies, resulting in enormous savings through reduced time, errors, and personnel costs (often while also improving the customer experience and overall performance.) Robotic process automation, for example, is able to cut policy conversion time by 50 percent for insurance companies while one large financial institution used RPA to reduce processing costs by 80 percent.

Trim the excess

We have found that in most organizations, general and administration expenses (G&A) and personnel are likely to yield the biggest cost-saving opportunities. The most effective personnel savings are based on rethinking processes and ways you work as well as revisiting strategic priorities, rather than simply letting go of people. When done correctly, best-in-class businesses reduce overlaps in activities, eliminate inefficiencies, and focus personnel on growth activities. One consumer-goods company readjusted its strategy to focus on customer service and innovation, allowing it to cut back on capabilities that didn't support those specific capabilities. This led to roughly 20 percent in savings in personnel costs. But cuts must be approached with care. G&A includes some critical activities, such as enabling innovation and developing talent. When done correctly, however, the impact can be profound. One global chemical company invested substantial effort in identifying discrete cost-saving opportunities across functions, tracking performance and involving hundreds of employees company-wide. It succeeded in reducing G&A by more than 20 percent within one year and sustaining its improvements for more than three years thereafter. In all, the company realized savings of well over $100 million and earnings before interest, taxes, and amortization (EBITDA) margin improvements of about three percentage points over two years, and then sustained it.

2. Find and fund the opportunities

The most successful companies prioritize the opportunities they uncover so that they can quickly allocate funds and people to them as they become available. Those opportunities generally come in two flavors: first are proven winners—existing programs that could outperform with greater investment. The second are promising new areas that require funding to acquire or launch. A good example of the first is when Geico dug deep into the return on its marketing spend and found that advertising drove the fastest growth. So over the course of 15 years, it tripled its marketing budget—and increased market share by 150 percent, in essence pulling money out of underperforming programs to fund a proven growth engine. For other companies, the growth drivers will be different; the important thing is to find what drives growth for *your* company—and fund it.

To be ready to allocate funds quickly to the most promising opportunities, successful companies take the following steps:

Identify and fund the high-potential opportunities

Most companies have plenty of data on hand to pinpoint the areas of greatest potential. This should yield insights both on where to invest for immediate growth and where investments are most likely to pay off over the long term. Former Comcast Cable CEO Neil Smit said that when he joined the company, it was selling over a million subscriptions a year to its high-speed data (HSD) service, yet HSD had received little investment. "It's a high-margin product. We're underpenetrated. That's the product we have to drive the hardest," Smit recalls. Chase took a similar approach when creating Sapphire Reserve, a credit card targeting affluent millennials, with a rich set of benefits (travel, experiences) to break through the clutter of the marketplace. The initial launch was so successful that Chase doubled down by cutting $200 million in selling, general and administrative (SG&A) costs to fund the benefits as they continued to expand the program. This effort led to 13 percent growth in the credit-card business in 2017, with Reserve cardholders spending six times more than the industry average. As companies search for opportunities, they should also mine their frontline workers, who can be an important source of intelligence on trends and opportunities. Many businesses find it helpful to create an "opportunity map" of potentially lucrative hot spots. The best companies, however, run advanced analytics against internal and external data sets from a variety of sources to build a picture of the future opportunity, not the historical reality.

Reallocate funds and people dynamically

High-performing Investor companies have mastered the art of dynamic allocation. Research from McKinsey shows that dynamic reallocators, those that reallocate at least 49 percent of the previous year's budget, achieve a compound annual growth rate in total return to shareholders of 10 percent, compared with just 6.1 percent for static allocators. Roughly 57 percent of companies in the top quartile for growth actively manage their portfolios based on ROI, according to a recent McKinsey survey. And it's not just about putting funds to use; it's about focusing your best talent on where the growth is. One digital healthcare business credits effectively allocating people's time with making the difference between a 60 percent growth rate and one that's 20 percent. Effective allocation, however, requires discipline to follow through and a clear set of metrics that decision makers are aligned around. Leadership alignment on priority markets, in fact, is the top Investor activity for top-quartile growth companies.

Fund a continuous, systematic stream of acquisitions.

Programmatic M&A can be a powerful lever for growth. Companies that use it well invest up to 30 percent of their market cap each year in acquisitions that mesh with their strengths. To do that, however, requires constant work to maintain a healthy pipeline of target companies. Corning, for example, did due diligence on an average of 20 companies per year and made an average of five bids to maintain its pace of three acquisitions per year. This approach helped it to break out of the middle tier in its sector to become a top grower.

Be disciplined in prioritizing opportunities

To keep the process untainted by bias or territorial thinking, it must be rigorous and transparent, taking into account both the opportunities and the needs of the organization as a whole. One leading CPG set up a "global reinvestment council" of more than 20 leaders from across countries, regions, and functions to review business priorities against investment ideas and to make the tough calls on whether to focus on new ventures or pour funds into existing operations.

3. Embed the capabilities

To fund your own growth, disciplined decision making must become the new normal rather than a one-off exercise. Here are some critical steps to take:

Build a rigorous budgeting process

Rigor in budgeting requires clarity about current budget performance and a commitment to allocating spend to drive growth. Zero-based budgeting (ZBB), for example, requires teams to rebuild their annual budgets from zero, with no carryover from the previous year. This process helps to identify small and not-so-small pockets of waste that can add up to big savings. While it is common for budget owners to use bottom-up budgeting, for truly breakthrough results, they need systematic visibility into budgets, clarity about what to measure, accountability for ambitious targets, and governance mechanisms to challenge budgets and reallocate resources. As Lila Snyder, executive vice president and president of global e-commerce at Pitney Bowes, put it, "We've set pretty explicit metrics for each business around the types of margins and the types of investments that we're willing to make. It's been very important to have that in the background, because it's easy to get distracted one quarter to the next when you're seeing growth but maybe not seeing margin."

Build mechanisms to surface investment opportunities

Finding opportunities to save and reinvest requires engagement from across the enterprise, from finance experts to product owners to business-unit leaders. But while the spirit of cooperation may be strong, without dedicated mechanisms to surface opportunities, those good intentions often amount to little. A leading consumer company set up a "fighting fund" where internal sponsors can apply for investment, using a business case and proven ROI. The company implemented a quarterly application cycle, with requalification required at agreed upon stage-gates when teams must submit detailed business cases as part of their reapplication.

Support data-driven decision-making

Investors of any sort are only as effective as the data they rely on. Many bring in data scientists to set up a robust analytics capability. Once they identify the highest-potential areas for investment, they use analytics to develop a more granular view of where—and how—to double down, investigating by city, segment, region, product, or even demographics, using a mix of methods. One leading consumer company worked with artificial-intelligence specialist Spark Beyond to analyze hundreds of thousands of inputs. The analysis helped it to identify meta trends in the data that pointed to pockets of growth targeted down to the suburb, nationality, even family size. In developing effective analytics, it's important to focus on rationalizing data and creating common standards (for KPIs, metrics) so that investment performance across activities is comparable.

While operating like an Investor requires specific capabilities, the key differentiator is mind-set. Without a near-fanatical leadership commitment to continually squeeze money from existing programs and the discipline to invest in growth, companies will find themselves missing out on their potential.

Leadership in innovation needs innovation in leadership

As businesses face evolving challenges, four aspects of leadership will become dramatically more important: insight, integrity, courage, and agility.

It may be that **advancing technology** plays the most visible role in shaping manufacturing progress in the years ahead. But we believe that what will matter at least as much for manufacturing's future is something that's much less visible, even though it has long been the bedrock of performance: effective leadership. How individual leaders inspire and influence others will become a key differentiator between organizations that thrive and those that do not.

In our experience transforming large, complex organizations at scale, the bulk of the work is usually in creating operational and managerial solutions. Yet we also know that nothing will happen, let alone sustain itself over time, without effective leadership. Indeed, extensive—and remarkably quantitative—research confirms that there are roughly 20 fundamental components of leadership that correlate closely to organizational performance (exhibit).

Today's 20 research-supported traits support the four leadership characteristics our interviewees see as essential for the future.

- Facilitate group collaboration
- Solve problems efficectively
- Make quality decisions   1. Insight
- Offer a critical perspective
- Communicate prolifically and enthusiastically

- Role model organizational values
- Give praise
- Be supportive   2. Integrity
- Develop others
- Foster mutual respect

- Remain composed and confident in uncertainty
- Keep group organized and on task
- Operate with strong results orientation
- Develop and share collective mission   3. Courage
- Seek different perspectives
- Champion desired change

- Recover positively from failures
- Clarify ojectives, rewards, and consequences
- Motivate and bring out best in others   4. Agility
- Differentiate among followers

We know that the list is hardly set in stone, and that what we define today as leadership is only one necessary part of organizational health. Yet what excites us about the list is that while some of the 20 may be seem almost self-explanatory (for example, "solve problems effectively"), collectively they actually work.

This foundation in hand, we recently interviewed colleagues with experience across a wide range of manufacturing environments, asking them what they saw as the next domains of great leadership. We all agreed that it's impossible (and likely counterproductive) to define all the answers here; future leadership will evolve rapidly and unpredictably. But those conversations nevertheless form a call to action showing where leadership must progress in order to support change and innovation.

We found that while the 20 fundamentals will likely remain essential, manufacturers will need even more effective leadership to withstand the unavoidable forces pressing change on every level:

- The multidecade explosion in new materials, innovative process technology, labor-displacing robotics and automation, predictive-analytic tools, and vast data pools, which are now predicted to reach 180 zettabytes around the world by 2025.

- The evolution of supertransparent supply markets that have enabled widespread cleansheet costing and produced unprecedented challenges in defining products' design attributes, cost, and pricing. At the same time, as oceans, trade barriers, and longstanding relationships recede in importance, transparent buying markets constantly raise customers' standards around the world.

- The rise of "employee experience" in a workforce that rightly looks for more engagement, support, inclusion, and coaching and is increasingly able to draw critical comparisons with other work environments, leaders, and even industries.

- Highly dynamic political currents in which manufacturing has assumed a new prominence in policy makers' agendas.

Against this context, we believe the fundamental profile of personal and organizational leadership is about something more than the important basics. Four attributes will enable individuals and organizations to stand out and move forward at a distinctive pace. Effective leaders will have the *insight* to clearly see and calibrate what really matters in operations and people; the *integrity* to build deep wells of trust and conviction; the *courage* to take on really tough opportunities quickly; and the *agility* to know when they need to shift course and move on. The four build on one another: when we see opportunity clearly, we need to trust each other in committing to take bold action and know that we can adapt and overcome unforeseen barriers. A leader —or, better still, an entire organization of leaders—that can combine all four well can do great things.

Insight

In our interviews, we encountered a number of closely related stories about discipline, concentration, and persistent tracking of value. Great operational leaders have an incisive sense of what matters and the ability to see constant sources of opportunity (and resistance) relative to that objective.

Dedication to value and performance can help an organization constantly orient toward the next opportunity, without getting distracted by pure novelty. This ability quickly gets an organization moving with confidence. One basic-materials company executive "had a completely instinctive sense" of the areas of performance that would fuel a rapid turnaround —targeting the uptime and reliability of specific heavy equipment, a positive trend in water and energy demand, and sustaining high safety performance.

At the best organizations, this disciplined sense of direction cascades powerfully to the front line: one of the authors of this article will never forget standing in a major automotive stamping line, listening to three hourly team members energetically describe how they cracked a millimeter-level defect in the stamping of an entire car-body panel. Or an example from a major healthcare player suffering from a quality compliance shock. Once the storm passed, the organization had the wonderfully stubborn discipline to return right back to the long-range productivity and cost-performance focus its leaders had championed, recognizing that far from conflicting, the cost and quality imperatives reinforced one another.

Integrity

In our work, we live in the thick of major transformations that push organizations and teams to their limits. Invariably, the programs that succeed have high-integrity leaders who model behaviors and decisions and are relentlessly consistent to their declared aspirations: on safety, productivity, or any other objective. These leaders stay true to organizational values, commitments, and each other, and they build deep wells of confidence and trust that add tremendous strength to the organization.

This "trust dividend" inspires and earns the respect of the people, who will stay the course even in tough times and accomplish great things. The dividend's value is most obvious when things are not going well—after the exciting start gives way to the long sustainment, for instance. This genuine integrity builds organizational resilience.

At the critical point in the transformation of a basic-materials company, an executive site manager gave up her top role to personally lead a transformation that many in the company had dismissed as "just another program." She recognized a moment of truth, took what was arguably a lower-rank role, cleaned out her office, and handed the keys to a more-junior leader. This was a clear act of self-sacrifice and a very real professional risk. Had the transformation failed under her leadership, she would have had no easy path to reinstatement. Her actions confirmed what she had been saying was the most important priority—the transformation. By taking the role of change-program leader, in a traditional organization that valued classic line-leadership roles, she strongly reinforced the transformation story.

High-integrity leaders also demonstrate a great personal generosity and humility, identifying their own personal success or a subordinate's lapse as something "we did." Such leaders also regularly demonstrate authentic caring and interest in their team—almost as a head of a family, speaking and acting with a distinctly personal sense of duty to their team members.

Courage

Courageous leaders demonstrate bold, informed risk taking and the grit to persist in the face of challenges. They impel the organization forward, accepting uncertainty and taking on major stretches of hard work in areas that show potential for real reward—and, more seriously, real risk of loss as well. It is the ethos of doing "the harder right instead of the easier wrong."

In the basic-materials case, the courageous act was a determination not only to invest publicly in a major review of water use and impacts across all sites but also to publicly reach out to environmental organizations that had criticized the company. It would have been far easier to hold back, run the operation as is, and react only to a failure event.

It's also important to distinguish bold ideas, in the pure-innovation sense that's so visible in high tech, from bold application of those ideas in an actual business. Innovation is important; making big moves based on innovation, including decisions that may involve long-term and even irreversible outcomes, is another matter. Ford's dramatic decision to convert its global best-selling vehicle, the F-Series pickup trucks, from industry-standard steel to aluminum, illustrates the point well. Ford changed far more than a material: it changed its supply-chain structure, its tooling, its procedures, and its entire workforce experience. We saw a similar story at a heavy-vehicle manufacturer that made a bold bet on an entirely different assembly process that, counterintuitively, increased its flexibility and speed.

While most organizations will eventually progress toward better, more advanced ideas, it is speed that sets some apart. We see too many examples of cautious leadership creating long, multiyear gaps between the recognition of a great idea and real adoption. Successful organizations also have the grit to move beyond the idea or the proof-of-concept pilot to implementing at scale.

Boeing provides a great example in its adoption of moving assembly lines for whole-aircraft manufacturing. Traditionally, airplanes were built in single, old-school stations, absent much of the rigor typical of high-volume assembly lines in the automotive sector. The idea of moving lines in aircraft assembly took hold in the late 1990s for the comparatively low-volume Boeing 717. Boeing then adapted the idea to its core 737 production lines, and then to the far more complex production of the 777. Testing a moving line is hard work, and deploying a new operations model takes courage—the kind of bold path that might not normally be taken.

A similar path is currently unfolding at SpaceX, whose Falcon rockets and Dragon capsule spacecraft have already helped dramatically reduce the cost of orbital delivery. Yet aggressive levels of design cost targeting are just part of the story, which also relies on major progress in new technologies such as advanced friction-stir welding, and a determination to in-source virtually the entire production process at US wage rates. The company's willingness to absorb substantial risks and recover quickly from setbacks has thus far kept it on track to achieve its ambitious mission of launching humans—potentially to Mars.

Agility

Great military leaders recognize that no plan, regardless of preparation, survives first contact: "the enemy always gets a vote." The world is under zero obligation to conform to any leader's strategy. Great leaders and organizations have the humility, situational awareness, and organizational skills to adapt to the world as it is and as it evolves. They combine flexibility with a disciplined ability to look down-range to see real and imagined bumps in the road, both threats and opportunities.

Retired astronaut Fred Haise, one of three flight crew on Apollo 13, recently shared an experience. On April 14, 1970, the crew's moon mission aborted when a cryogenic oxygen tank exploded, catastrophically disabling the vital Service Module spacecraft. The odds on a safe return were extremely long.

Haise spoke about the apparent lack of contingency plans and the now-famous problem-solving struggle to bring his crew home. He was clear: the reason there was no backup plan was not because someone hadn't imagined the failure—it was because NASA had determined this type of event to be nonsurvivable. Haise's personal story is an iconic example of agile leadership: a team adapting to the world as it is and not as they planned it to be. The team demonstrated the humility necessary to discard an original, deeply invested plan; oriented itself quickly (in a matter of minutes) to a new situation; adapted; and overcame. Agile leaders hold fast to a clear intent (value, innovation, or any other goal) but quickly and intelligently create new plans that rely on new insights, better ideas, and *more reality*. Like that Apollo flight crew, they constantly solve problems and keep going.

From four to more

Insight, integrity, courage, and agility—backed by the 20 fundamentals—will help serve as the practical navigational points for innovative future leadership. While there are no textbook answers to what this will look and feel like, a few essential questions can help organizations begin to think about what they will need of their leaders:

1. How can a leader and a team create the space, mindfulness, innovative relationships, and objectivity that foster insight?

2. What can build our integrity, trust, and a moral and professional sense of purpose of who we are, what we do, and why we are so deeply committed?

3. What can increase our courage to confront tough situations and high-risk opportunities positively, even amid genuine fear?

4. What will allow us to see, understand, and rapidly recalibrate to a shifting landscape in ways that progressively challenge our people?

Much of what will be called innovation will actually be the recycling and rediscovery of existing ideas—perhaps in digital or even robotically supported formats. But that adaption is itself an innovation worth doing. Whatever form it takes, the next horizon of operations leadership will increase the velocity of organizational performance, particularly in the deeply technological, high-stakes and (still) very human environment of 21st century manufacturing.

Four ways the best sales teams beat the market

Top-performing sales leaders know that the traditional metrics for evaluating sales ROI aren't always adequate for the new complexity of digital and multichannel selling.

M anaging large sales forces has never been easy for multinational companies. However, increasing competition, margin pressure, the rise of digital and proliferating channels have added a significant layer of complexity. Already today nearly a third of all B2B purchases are done digitally while customers use an average of six channels for prospecting, forcing sales leaders to rethink how they source leads, manage pipelines, and sell more effectively.

Rather than being overwhelmed, the best sales leaders have figured out how to overcome this complexity to drive above-market growth. Our analysis of 73 B2B technology companies shows that across sectors, the top 25 percent of companies achieve a better than 2× higher sales ROI compared to the bottom 25 percent.

What do they do right? Based on our experience and analysis, they maintain a clear focus on four things:

1. They understand what really matters

The key to smart investing is having good data that highlights where the greatest sales ROI is. That starts by knowing what to measure. Many companies, however, measure sales efficiency in terms of sales cost versus revenue. That metric is misleading because it does not sufficiently reflect the margin differences between sales channels. A more meaningful sales ROI is to measure sales cost against gross margin or profit (EBIT).

This sales ROI metric helps leaders more effectively align the number of accounts per sales employee with actual and potential revenues. By analyzing the sales ROI potential of various segments, for example, sales leaders uncover different channel approaches for each. In one company, analysis revealed that sales ROI in indirect channels was 50 percent greater than in direct channels.

The best leaders also achieve such high sales ROI by reducing overall sales costs without giving away too much margin. Approaches include a strong "quality instead of quantity" focus on their highest-performing partners. They also tend to de-emphasize direct discounts, such as rebates and product offerings.

2. They don't waste money

While the old addage "It takes money to make money" is popular, it's not true when it comes to the best sales leaders. The best of them keep their costs lower than their peers do. Consider that 72 percent of companies in the top quartile of sales ROI also have the lowest sales costs. Effectively controlling costs requires a clear and objective view of profitability and cost-to-sell by channel, product, and customer.

With this foundation, sales leaders can make better decisions, such as scaling back sales efforts for lower-value orders. They also invest in processes and training that cut costs, such as installing technologies that reduce the number of order exceptions and cross-training people to have multiple skills. This level of efficiency not only reduces costs but also allows sales leaders to profitably pursue lower-margin business.

3. They free up their salespeople for selling

Top-performing sales organizations have the same percentage of sales staff in sales management roles—around 8 percent—as lower-performing companies. However, they have about 30 percent more sales staff in *support* roles. While this may seem counterintuitive, this approach frees up sales reps from more administrative tasks, such as order management and developing sales collateral, and allows them to devote more of their time to customers. The result is that frontline sales reps are three times more productive than their peers.

One leading high-tech-equipment business, for example, found that 28 percent of sales-rep time was spent on low-value activities like handling complaints. They then shifted about half of these transactional activities into a sales factory and freed up 13 percent of sales reps' time for selling.

Sales executives also need to take a hard look at their sales support systems. Some activities can be automated or streamlined, some can be delegated and pooled into back-office sales factories, and others can be cut entirely. Implementing such operational and structural changes requires a clear understanding of just what constitutes low- versus high-value-add activities and what resources are currently devoted to each.

4. They are adept at multichannel selling

Companies that effectively sell across multiple channels (inside sales, outsourced agents, value-added resellers, third-party retail stores, distributors, or wholesalers) achieve more than 40% higher sales ROI than companies wedded to a single channel model (only key account management and/or field sales). Managing multiple channels calls for effectively addressing selling opportunities based on value versus on volume, and recognizing that not every channel is optimal for every product. For instance, *inside* sales reps can handle key accounts with low-complexity products, whereas more costly in-person support should be assigned exclusively to key accounts with high-complexity products.

How does this work in practice? An IT hardware producer had seen declining profitability and rising sales costs in its main business unit. It started by benchmarking performance in the sales organization and discovered that its sales ROI of 2.6 was far below the industry median of 3.5.

The company decided it needed to do a better job getting its sales force to focus on growth opportunities. It developed a new customer segmentation based on revenue and opportunity rather than global accounts, commercial accounts, and small and medium-sized businesses. Aligning sales coverage accordingly, the company devoted more resources to higher-value segments, i.e., those with higher revenue and higher future opportunity, and reduced coverage for accounts with lower revenue and opportunity.

Benchmarking its global business across five divisions and three regions also revealed significantly higher sales costs compared to its peers. The company examined its channels, including a direct sales force, distributors, and online channels. The direct channel captured higher gross margins (40 percent) than the distributor channel (35 percent). However, sales costs were higher too: 20 percent versus 12 percent of revenue. To ensure that the higher direct-channel spend generated the greatest possible return, the company matched different sales people to various customer segments, based on their purchasing profile. Leadership assigned a dedicated sales person to each of the most important global accounts. A dedicated sales rep served 5 – 10 of the next tier of customers, while lower value customers were served by inside sales or the web. This allowed the company to achieve the best match between actual and potential revenues on the one hand and sales costs on the other. To reduce costs, they replaced excess specialist channel managers with less expensive generalist managers in affected business units. This approach yielded an expected 5-10% productivity gain (~USD 150-300m).

Many companies are understandably afraid to "tinker with" sales, the only part of the organization that actually brings in the revenue. We believe, however, that more aggressive action to match sales resources with sales ROI opportunities is critical if companies are looking to beat the market.

Setting an agenda for organic growth in the digital age

Business leaders can focus on three mind-sets to drive growth in their companies and sustain that growth for the long term.

E xecutives who make growth their priority and ambitiously set goals and invest based on that intent are often more successful in growing their businesses. In this episode of the *McKinsey Podcast*, McKinsey partner Kabir Ahuja and senior partner Liz Hilton Segel speak with McKinsey's Barr Seitz about how a company can increase its growth rate using three different mind-sets, or lenses, to direct its strategy.

Podcast transcript

Barr Seitz: Hello. And welcome to the *McKinsey Podcast*. I'm Barr Seitz, global publishing lead for McKinsey's Marketing & Sales and Digital practices. And I'm very happy to be joined by Kabir Ahuja, a partner, and Liz Hilton Segel, a senior partner who leads the Marketing & Sales Practice in the Americas. They are also the coauthors of the article, "Invest, Create, Perform: Mastering the three dimensions of growth in the digital age," which was published in March. In today's conversation we'll be digging into the importance of organic growth, how the best companies approach it, and what they do to change their growth trajectories. Liz and Kabir, thank you very much for joining us today.

Kabir Ahuja: Happy to be here.

Liz Hilton Segel: Thank you.

Barr Seitz: Liz, let's start with you. In getting ready for this conversation, I reread a few McKinsey articles on growth. There was one in 1996 called, "Staircases to growth," which looked at how the top growers took a systematic series of manageable steps rather than single bold leaps to sustain growth.

Then in 2007, there was the article, "The granularity of growth," based on the book of the same title. It argued that companies can unlock significant growth by identifying, at very narrow and small market segments, where demand is strongest. So the topic of growth isn't new. What is new about growth?

Liz Hilton Segel: Digital has changed a lot about how companies compete for their consumers and their customers. Competition is higher than ever because digital and the internationalization of markets make consumer expectations and the fighting for consumers and customers more intense than they've ever been.

It really leads to pressure on companies to make sure that their products and services, and their customer experiences, are truly at the cutting edge of the industry to ensure that they're getting their fair share of revenues in the marketplace. But digital and advanced analytics also offer opportunities for companies. We are seeing people leverage real-time data in very, very new ways to make better decisions on how they price, where they invest, and where they apply their sales force. While, on the one hand, digital is offering the threat that if you don't keep up, you're unlikely to retain your market-share position, it's also offering an opportunity to extract even more value by innovating your commercial processes.

What we've seen is that, as the financial markets have increasingly put pressure on executives to deliver earnings in a very consistent way, there's been more and more company focus on cost and cost containment. Certainly that's partially driven by a slow GDP growth globally. But our questions are, "Can you really pivot to more of a growth agenda? And can you leverage some of the cost savings that you've developed skills in to invest further in the company's growth?" Ultimately, that's a better path to value creation. Our point of view is that growth really matters both to company value creation but also to company survival.

If you look, you'll find that over half the companies on the New York Stock Exchange that did not grow didn't survive. And so it absolutely is a priority. When we look at our clients, and other institutions, we really have faith and confidence that people can grow more. What we would do is invite them to explore the question of, "What would it take to increase the company's growth rate?" Because with focus and a disciplined attempt at it, we're really confident that the company's growth rate can be more than what it's been.

Barr Seitz: Great. Kabir, you led a body of research into how the best companies approach growth in the digital age. What were some of the highlights of that research?

Kabir Ahuja: We talked to a large number of executives to learn how they think about growth, how they approach growth, and how historically their companies had created and delivered growth. What we found out was, first of all, one of the key markers of a successful growth agenda is having a senior leadership team that has the intent to grow. They actively think about growth as a top management item and invest behind it.

Then we have a separate set of learnings, which is about the *how*. We learned that there were three lenses that companies use to drive growth. One is performance, which is easily understood. It's improving the operational and commercial engines to increase sales and channel performance.

There's a second, which is creation. That creator lens is all about generating new revenue through new products and services. Then there's the investor lens, which is all about reallocating your resources the right way and taking money away from, and resources from, parts of the business that aren't returning well, so that you're not starving places where there's opportunity to grow. We found that the best growers use all three lenses.

Barr Seitz: Great. This idea of corporate dexterity to pursue a diversified approach to growth makes sense. I think you'd expect companies to be able to walk and chew gum at the same time, to oversimplify the point. So, Liz, why is this diversified approach to growth important? And what would a CEO or business-unit leader do differently because of this insight?

Liz Hilton Segel: One thing, just to start with, is, as an executive, to simply ask yourself the question, "Which strategies do I tend toward?" My experience working with clients across a lot of companies is that executives, as individuals, and management teams really do tend to bias.

There are certain things that they are more comfortable with, that they know have worked for them, and so they'll tend to stay on that strategy for a longer period of time. They will see it as risky to step out beyond that. If you bring ten executives together, and you describe to them the three lenses of growth, and you ask them to describe [themselves], very quickly people will say, "Oh, well, I'm performer oriented," or, "I'm investor oriented," or, "I'm creator oriented."

People can self-diagnose quite easily. The question on our minds is if you're quite deliberate about trying to broaden your capability set as a company and then to take a step back and say, "What do we want to aspire to as a growth rate? What do I think our industry's producing? If I try to aspire to grow at a rate in excess of the industry, and I try to adopt a broader or more diversified tool kit, what would I do differently than I'm doing today?"

Kabir Ahuja: That's one of the hardest questions that I see, at least in all of my conversations, is, "How fast should I be growing?" It's a fundamentally hard thing to understand what your trajectory is and how much you can affect it.

Barr Seitz: How do you answer that question? I'm assuming it's very difficult.

Liz Hilton Segel: We try to take both a top-down and a bottom-up approach to it. So the top-down point of view simply is, "Let's look at your industry segment. Let's look at the degree to which you are weighted to the faster- or the slower-growing parts of your industry segment." Then create a natural growth trajectory based on the momentum of the industry.

The bottom-up approach to it is to take each of these lenses—investor, creator, performer— and say at a granular level, "What do we think the opportunities are for your company? And what's holding you back from achieving those opportunities to create a road map?"

Kabir Ahuja: Often it ends up with an aspiration for growth that is greater than when they start. That's really the mind-set shift that we encourage senior executives to take, especially those who can control those multiple lenses—to have a growth aspiration and be oriented around it.

Barr Seitz: Did you ever see that movie *The Candidate* with Robert Redford? It's about a candidate running for the US Senate. He gets caught up in the campaigning, and he forgets what he's running for. And then he wins. There's this great scene at the end when he talks to his campaign manager and asks him, "All right. What do we do now?"

As a CEO looking at this framework—creator, performer, investor—and they're ready to develop that corporate dexterity to pursue a diversified growth program, but what do we do now? Kabir, how does an executive turn this organic growth map into a functioning operating model for growth?

Kabir Ahuja: You have to start with being deliberate about creating a plan for how to grow using the different lenses and then, on the back of that, have a sequence and understand the capabilities you need.

An example company: for the investor portion, we found there were actual cities that were ripe for expansion into. From the creator lens, we said, "Look, there's a lot of innovation in entertainment and the bar and restaurant scene." The value proposition could actually ratchet up their revenue by a significant amount if you could find two or three more opportunities for patrons to spend and be happy.

Then from the performer lens, their sales channels didn't have the required level of performance management that they needed. We had a clear sense in each of the three lenses where growth could come from. Then on the back end, you have to think about what capabilities you need, what you have, and the speed to impact of each of those activities and sequence them in the right order.

Barr Seitz: This idea of being deliberate I just find intriguing because it seems so simple.

Kabir Ahuja: It does. We had a CFO forum in London. We had 100 of the world's leading CFOs, and we talked about this. It was funny because, in reflection, many of them said, "Oh, yeah, we're definitely a performer." Then you ask the question, "Well, was that on purpose, or is it just what you're comfortable doing?"

Oftentimes the answer is, "It's what we're comfortable doing." And that's fine. They happen to be very good at it, and it's delivered a lot of value. But then you run out of juice at some point. You need to diversify the tactics you use. Liz, I'm sure you've seen this with your clients. There's a way to consciously choose to do something else and build the capabilities to make sure it succeeds.

Liz Hilton Segel: What's hard about it, and often why a new executive can create the shake-up necessary to reset the growth agenda, is that, certainly in the case of being an investor, odds are you're going to break glass as it relates to how the budget has been spent in the past.

You're going to go in and say, "Hey, we need to find a way to spend less money here in order to spend more money there. We're in a performer mind-set. There's actually a better way to do this. And we're going to deliberately build new skills to optimize our pricing approach or to squeeze more efficiency out of our marketing spend." By definition, what we're asking for is change. And we're asking for change in the service of higher company performance on the growth dimension.

Barr Seitz: Liz, when we've talked about this idea of having a diversified approach to growth, you've mentioned companies performing like triathletes, where they have to build up different sets of muscles to be able to do multiple things well. What sorts of muscles do businesses need to develop to drive growth? And how do they balance the development of them to do those three things well?

Liz Hilton Segel: Kabir referred to this earlier, but you have to decide to be in the race. You have to decide that you're there to play and that you're there to play a growth game. And you need to get the whole management team lined up behind a growth game.

When we start talking about growth, sometimes people think this is a CEO question because it's a strategy question. Sometimes people think, "Oh, this is the CMO's question," because it's about how to spend your marketing dollars. Or sometimes people think, "Oh, it's the head of the sales force," because they're the ones who create revenue for the business.

But in reality it's the entire management team's question, and the CFO plays about as valuable a role as anybody because ultimately they're a major part of the question of how resources are allocated. I would say the first thing, absolutely table stakes, is a mind-set that, "We are here as a management team to deliver a faster growth rate than we have in the past."

The second thing is a very disciplined resource-allocation process —and whether that's about net new, meaning that there's always a point of view in the company about where to spend dollars on the margin and clarity about what those dollars will return, or whether that's a mental model that says no individual budget item is held because it was last year's number. There's always opportunity to squeeze out more savings in a company. The reason why is because, if you don't do that, there's an opportunity cost relative to where new investments might be placed to get incremental growth.

Beyond those two, what we found is that folks who were top growers had two capabilities that really stood out relative to their peers who were not growing as fast.

One was, not surprisingly, around data and analytics. That might be a marker of what companies today who are really leaning forward—what are they investing capabilities in? We certainly see data and analytics as something that helps you squeeze out incremental growth on the margin. Then the second thing is the ability to collaborate cross-functionally to work in an agile method; this is another marker of top growers.

We didn't see things like innovation per se as something that particularly differentiated top growers from others, which I think is interesting. We did see, for the different lenses we talked about, for companies that self-identified as a creator, that customer insights was something that they also called out as being unique to them. Within the investor, we found that they identified speed and efficiency in their processes as something that was a particular competency of their organization.

Barr Seitz: When we talk about data and analytics, there's a sense that that's all about productivity. How do you think about that as a growth-tool capability?

Kabir Ahuja: Understanding this whole resource-allocation question, it's not just a process question. It's also a data question. It's, "How well can I understand the cells of performance?"—whether it be by channel, by geography, by type of sales force. There are so many ways you can cut data in your business.

This is back to the articles that you talked about. The principles are still applied today: granularity of growth—understanding where to put your dollars to find growth. Data can be a huge accelerator to that and make a real difference.

Similarly, you can use data and analytics in insight. We now have empirical views on how people interact with the world because of digital. It is really powerful to not just use data as a back-end "How did things go?" but actually understand how the world works around you, how your customers experience your products or services, or even interactions with you, and then use that to go back into this whole creator mind-set.

Liz Hilton Segel: In general, when we work with clients to help them either change their capabilities or to achieve a higher level of performance, our experience is that the two go hand in hand best. In other words, if you're a company and you say, "Look, I'm sitting here with a 3 percent growth rate, and I want to be at a 6 percent growth rate," and you believe that data and analytics is the path to that, we will of course bring in people that have data and analytics expertise. That's certainly very helpful to a client to pave out where they want to go.

But more important is applying that to a specific set of initiatives that are going to produce the higher growth rate, so that the building of the data and analytics capability is fueling the outcome you want, and then it's completely self-reinforcing.

Kabir Ahuja: One of the biggest things about data analytics is it gives you the capability to respond much quicker. It's data analytics both in terms of level of precision, using machine learning and a whole bunch of new techniques, but also the speed at which it happens has changed dramatically how the actions a company can take on the back end happen.

Barr Seitz: And why is that so important today?

Kabir Ahuja: Well, everybody's moving faster. If you have a new product, you can expect a fast follower faster than ever before.

Liz Hilton Segel: If I think about one of my retail clients who is now just beginning the journey of using real-time competitive pricing information to change their promotional decisions every day on every SKU, the concept of that seems very daunting at first. But once you actually get moving on it, you can always make it incrementally better.

Barr Seitz: Liz, you've alluded to this in our conversation earlier, in terms of the mind-set that executives need to have to drive growth. Having worked with business leaders on growth and observed how the most successful ones operate, what are the characteristics of leading executives who can drive growth consistently?

Liz Hilton Segel: The first thing is just to set an ambitious agenda around growth and to be as purposeful about going after that growth agenda as you might after a cost transformation or a reengineering or restructuring effort.

The company needs to have the leadership of the CEO or the business-unit head. It needs a purposeful set of initiatives, and it needs a clear path to go after achieving those initiatives. So the first thing simply is, set the agenda and do it in a disciplined way.

The second thing I would note is that it is really helpful to be thinking concurrently about the short term and the long term. Sometimes growth conversations can have an ethereal feel, like we're talking about several years from now. While it's absolutely important to put investments down today and to go after innovation that may not produce for a couple of years, there's no question that that's valued. There needs to be a balance with things that will really deliver and produce results in the short term.

The last thing is, look closely at results. You want to make sure that you're seeing material improvements quarter over quarter, whether it's to build momentum within the analyst community or whether it's to build momentum around the employee base, to build confidence in greater investment going forward, look closely at results.

Kabir Ahuja: The only thing I would add to that is that senior executives who are driving growth have the opportunity to set a story that the company can rally around and genuinely create excitement around growth. Growth is an exciting thing. One of the characteristics of the CEOs and business leaders and executives who execute growth successfully is that they set that growth story for the company and rally everyone behind it.

Barr Seitz: To get to the next level down, what does that look like to set a growth agenda? What does it look like to review results and take decisions based on that?

Liz Hilton Segel: My view is it looks like any planning process in the company. It is an end-to-end review of every opportunity for growth that is in the company. It might go business unit by business unit. It might go function by function. But it's the disciplined asking of the question, "Where can we get more?"

Whether that's, "Where can we get more from what we do today?"—the way we talked about through the performer lens. Or whether that's, "Where is there a white space in a market that we are not yet seizing?"—and therefore you look at it through the creator lens and say, "What is a part of the market we want to actually play in? And what are our ideas about what products or services might play in those markets?" Or whether it's the question around the investor, which is, "If I had another hundred million dollars, where would I deploy it?" And now let me go ask the question of, "Where am I going to get that hundred million dollars?" Like any planning process, it's just a disciplined look across the company. It's just with an expectation of an outcome, which is an acceleration of the company's growth rate.

Kabir Ahuja: And just to pair with that: discipline tracking.

Liz Hilton Segel: Yes.

Kabir Ahuja: It's the disciplined look about where we're going to grow and then tracking if you're delivering that growth against the identified areas. So much like what Liz said, it's like any other structured process, and growth can be delivered that way.

Liz Hilton Segel: It just comes back to the message that we started with. If you go through and put in one group our clients who grow very rapidly, and another group our clients who do not, and you ask, "What's the top management priority?," the differentiator is what they're focused on. For the companies that are not growing, it's because their agenda is around cost or their agenda is around something else. For the companies that are growing, it's because that's the top management unit's objective.

Barr Seitz: I'm afraid we're out of time. Thank you, Liz and Kabir, for joining me for this conversation.

Kabir Ahuja: Thank you.

Liz Hilton Segel: Thank you.

Barr Seitz: As a reminder, you can read their article, "Invest, Create, Perform: Mastering the three dimensions of growth in the digital age," on McKinsey.com. And you can keep up with the latest from McKinsey on organic growth by following us on Twitter, @McK_MktgSales. Thank you for joining us today.

Reinventing the organization for faster growth

MásMóvil has been able to accelerate its growth by fostering a culture focused on growth and killing off emails, among other things.

In this interview, McKinsey's Dennis Spillecke talks to MásMóvil CEO Meinrad Spenger about the company's approach to growth. Launched in 2006, MásMóvil is now a top four telecommunications operator in Spain, serving eight million customers and generating nearly €1.5 billion in revenue in 2018.

What is your approach to faster growth?

If you want to go faster, you have to revise how the organization works, meaning not only processes but also the way people work. For instance, I try to eliminate most emails. This may seem provocative, but in a company where 85 percent of employees work in the same building, I want people to talk with each other; I don't want them to send long emails. Emails kill a lot of time, and sometimes they are just an excuse for someone to say, "I did my job." We don't want that.

In addition, a quick organization needs new agile ways of working. For us, it was a mind-set change from working in silos, in departments, to working in cross-functional teams, with the aim of delivering tangible results in the short term.

How do you empower your workforce with a growth mind-set?

If you want your company to grow, the first principle is to do everything to make your clients happy. Because if you have satisfied clients, then growth comes almost automatically.

In addition, you need a talented team and to enable a culture that fosters growth. This means quick decision making, no penalties if somebody does something wrong, meritocracy, no formalism, an 80/20 approach. Enable speed and quick decision making and foster new initiatives. I want MásMóvil to be full of entrepreneurs. I want people to take initiative.

Also very important is shareholder alignment. If our shareholders would not have had a clear idea that this is a growth story and they needed to support this growth, our growth would not have happened.

Almost nobody at MásMóvil has a big ego. We are a great team, and there is a good atmosphere, a good spirit, a good culture, no envies, support, good collaboration, and that produces great results. Look at the people who you are hiring for key positions. It's not so much about experience; it's a lot about attitude. Hire people that fit into your culture.

Can you learn about growth from the outside?

We challenge our team to see what we can learn from other sectors—for example, to uncover what our clients prefer as a service. And sometimes this can lead to things that are disruptive for our sector.

For example, we disrupted the process of installing fiber broadband connection in the homes of our Spanish clients. In the past, if you ordered broadband service, you needed to schedule an appointment for a technician to come to your house, and then you needed to take the day off work to wait for the technician to arrive. There was no interaction with the technician; you didn't know what time he would come, so there was a lot of frustration. So what we did is quite easy. We copied what apps such as Uber or mytaxi do, where we first send an exact appointment time to the client and then a link to the technician, so the client knows where the technician is, his name, his phone number, and then can coordinate with him. This was very easy to incorporate, and it was also very practical.

So being able to learn from other sectors is very important, because in terms of client experience, a lot of other sectors do it better than the telecom sector in general. For example, Netflix doesn't have a call center for customer care, so why do we need practically everything to be done in a call center? We try to learn from that. In two of our major brands, about 80 percent of the client interactions are already digital, and by the end of the year, it will likely be more than 90 percent. It's saving time, it's improving quality, it's increasing speed of incident resolution. It has a lot of advantages.

A tale of two agile paths: How a pair of operators set up their organizational transformations

Different approaches illustrate the company and market conditions that guide the structure of teams around work, and the rapid benefits that follow.

Although more than 70 percent of companies report that agile transformation is a top priority, we haven't seen the extent of agile adoption among operators that this level of interest would suggest. It's puzzling. We know companies that go agile are 50 percent likelier to outperform their competitors financially. We also know that agile directly helps operators win four of their core battles: faster time to market, higher customer satisfaction, significant productivity improvements, and a transformed employee experience that improves talent attraction and retention.

So, what is holding operators back?

We believe part of the answer is a lack of clarity about what "agility" actually means and how it plays out in practice within a specific company. The term is often used to connote a vague notion of being flexible. One executive explained his chronic lateness by saying he was just "being agile with time." Others associate the term with a type of software development or bean-bag chairs and flexible seating arrangements.

None of these definitions is accurate. What, then, is agility?

Exhibit 1

Agility is a shift in the model of what an organization is, and how it operates.

Organizations as **inflexible machines** to ... Next ❯

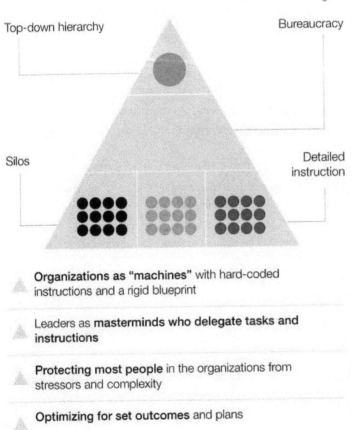

Top-down hierarchy

Bureaucracy

Silos

Detailed instruction

▲ **Organizations as "machines"** with hard-coded instructions and a rigid blueprint

▲ Leaders as **masterminds who delegate tasks and instructions**

▲ **Protecting most people** in the organizations from stressors and complexity

▲ **Optimizing for set outcomes** and plans

Think back to a crisis you were involved in or a time of urgent and decisive challenge. Maybe you were responding to an emergency in your community, serving in the military, or facing an impossible deadline at work. You assembled people from different backgrounds who were selected for their complementary skills, operated largely without hierarchy, and focused on a well-defined objective. These extraordinary achievements are often remembered as "peak experiences."

Agile, in a nutshell, is about assembling the elements of that peak experience for every employee, every day, without the need for a crisis. Agility at scale embeds these elements in the very fabric of how things are done by providing the following:

1. A very clear purpose, anchored in positive meaning

2. A sharp definition of what success looks like

3. Teams assembled with the skills required to succeed without reliance on others

4. A cadence that fosters short bursts of tangible output and regular celebration of outcomes

This is the core of agility—building organizations with hundreds of those great teams (Exhibit 1). However, great teams alone would result in chaos and lack of scale. The other critical piece is a strong backbone that supports these teams by providing a common purpose, cohesive culture, functional excellence, and standards, which in turn enable the processes and platforms that hold the company together.

Two approaches to agile

In our work with multiple operators around the globe, we have seen two successful approaches to agile emerge: agile accelerators and enterprise-wide agile (Exhibit 2). We'll use examples of agile in action at two different operators—Denmark's TDC and New Zealand's Spark—to demonstrate two emerging success patterns for how to organize teams around work. Both operators have reaped significant benefits through their transformation, including the four key benefits mentioned above, and attracted global attention in doing so. Telco executives from all over the world now visit both companies to learn how they changed long-held practices in favor of customer and operational excellence.

Exhibit 2

Two approaches to going agile have emerged.

Agile accelerators	What it is	The company profile	The approach	Telco example
	Establishes a number of agile units (tribes) to achieve immediate business benefit (eg, in digital)	• A need for rapid impact • Units that can be taken agile quickly are taken agile (most have) • Appetite to test the waters and learn what a wider agile transition requires	• Improve customer experience across core journeys • Reduce channel costs and go digital • Innovate core products	TDC
Enterprise-wide agile	Rebuilds the full organization around a radically delayered agile operating model	• Sound underlying performance and operational discipline • Strong core technology • Good adaptability and full top-team commitment to rapid and deep change	• Accelerate end-to-end product and customer-journey development • Increase employee engagement • Boost productivity across the business	Spark

The choice between the two approaches to agile is driven by how agility can best unlock value in a particular company, the maturity of the organization, and the top management team's convictions about starting small versus undertaking quick and comprehensive change. Common to both is the necessity for a company to be "all in" about agility—only the scope of initial change is different.

Next, we'll see how these two approaches played out at the geographical antipodes, TDC and Spark.

TDC: 'Digital first' first

The summer of 2016 was challenging for TDC, the leading Danish telco (see sidebar "About TDC"). The recent merger of its two main consumer brands had consolidated its B2C strategy and the newly appointed head of its B2C unit, Jaap Postma, had a long list of improvements to make in the new organization. TDC's digital capabilities were at the top of it—market research and Postma's own observations strongly suggested that the company was not meeting consumers' rising expectations of online service.

Having witnessed the power of digital in his previous positions, Postma set it as a top priority and tasked Rune Keldsen, one of his trusted leaders with broad, relevant experience, to get this right. Postma and Keldsen quickly concluded that doing things the old way would not produce results fast enough. TDC had invested significant funds in digital for years, but these efforts always tended to take longer than anticipated, and by the time they were ready to hit the market, consumer needs had often shifted already.

To speed things up, TDC decided to inject agility into its digital transformation. It first launched one, then 12 cross-functional agile teams (or squads) consisting of product owners, commercial specialists, frontline experts, customer-experience designers, architects, and developers—all the competencies required to design, build, test, and improve digital customer journeys at speed. Each squad was brought under the organizational construct of a "digital tribe" led by Keldsen. The squads were given end-to-end accountability to do whatever it took to create seamless and engaging customer journeys in online sales and service, while gradually establishing a flexible IT architecture.

Postma and Keldsen knew that to succeed with the digital transformation of TDC, they needed to establish a new culture and attract top talent. A casual walk-through of their Digital Warehouse shows they achieved this. At the facility, which is a rebuilt warehouse next to TDC headquarters, there is no more talking about business and IT, no more "facilitating" middle managers, and no more long steering-committee meetings. In their place are just cross-functional squads empowered to make change.

Eighteen months later, TDC sees the benefits of the new way of working. Its customer onboarding journey, for example, had been one of the main headaches for customers and a key reason for low satisfaction ratings. Post-transformation, TDC's onboarding experience is now endorsed with five stars by 80 percent of customers. Call volume, one of the large cost drivers for TDC, is down by more than 40 percent now that customers can easily manage their interactions and solve their problems online.

Online sales provide another striking example. Six months before the transformation began, TDC formed a traditional project team tasked with designing and implementing a new digital sales journey for the main products. But with team members located in disparate parts of the organization and working in a traditional waterfall approach, the project team hadn't managed to release *anything* by the time it was rolled into the digital tribe. Once they were co-located and equipped with agile techniques like minimum-viable-product thinking, the group had not only built a new sales journey but already generated its first online sales within a few weeks. The first minimum viable product was limited in scope, yet generated momentum, secured sponsorship, and bought the team time to deal with technical complexity of an automated solution that came a few months later. Conversion rates soared. The agile approach had worked.

After the groundbreaking success of the digital tribe in B2C, TDC immediately launched a similar digital tribe in B2B. This tribe is reinventing the sales and service experience for business customers and launching solutions that have not yet been seen elsewhere in the B2B space. Over the last six months TDC has continued to scale its new agile ways of working with three new tribes around digital marketing and product development (a TV tribe and a cloud tribe), all of which kicked off with success.

Spark New Zealand: 'Be agile to go agile'

Spark, New Zealand's incumbent operator, had been on a transformation journey since 2012, following the carving out of its fixed-access network to a separately listed new entity (see sidebar "About Spark"). Having completed a successful turnaround, rebranding, and IT reengineering, Spark was in good shape and shareholders enjoyed one of the sector's best total returns.

But the executive team was setting its sights higher. In their view, the game was no longer about outperforming other operators, but being match-fit for a market increasingly made of disruptive digital-native companies such as Amazon, Netflix, and Spotify. Competing or partnering with these companies requires a step-change in mind-set, speed of execution, and time to market, which the old functional organization model struggles to provide.

Armed with renewed urgency, Spark's top team and board of directors visited more than a dozen companies around the world to understand how agile worked for them and what it could do for Spark. They visited both born-agile companies and companies in different stages of their agile journey. These included, among others, TDC and ING in the Netherlands.

Spark leaders returned home with a simple conclusion: when it comes to agility, they needed to jump in boots and all, and trust the agile process to get them through—"be agile to go agile." They wanted to avoid a prolonged period in which part of the company had adopted agile ways of working and the rest was still operating in a traditional hierarchy. Companies that fully embraced agility across the organization were thriving. Those that just did it half-way often faced some difficulties. Spark likened this to a person on a dock standing with one foot on the ground and one foot on a boat.

Managing Director Simon Moutter and Group HR Director Joe McCollum called for a three-day off-site in October 2017 for the leadership team to decide if Spark would be in or out. The collective team pledged to adopt agile throughout the entire business, fast and at scale.

The team laid out an ambitious timeline to keep the transition phase to a minimum. In November 2017 Spark launched a company-wide communication about the upcoming journey and appointed leads to the first three tribes it launched as frontrunners: broadband, managed data, and digital experience. Over the following months, the leads of these three tribes built their own organization of about ten cross-functional teams each. In parallel, the rest of the organization prepared the changes needed to tip the whole company into an agile setup by mid-2018.

Along the way, Spark dedicated significant effort to change management and capability building. During the first half of 2018, well before any structural change occurred, hundreds of people engaged in defining and then putting into action a new purpose for the company: "Helping all of New Zealand win big in a Digital World." This new purpose brought about an adjustment in the company's values, target behaviors, and capabilities. They also emphasized diversity and inclusion so employees felt comfortable bringing their whole selves to work and working together, to ensure high performance in teams.

Operating in a small, remote market where talent with agile experience was hard to find, Spark selected 40 high-performing employees and trained them as agile coaches in a newly created academy. It also had all employees go through a two-day boot camp designed to build great teams familiar with the basics of agile.

In July 2018, Spark did a "big bang" launch of 18 tribes and moved approximately 40 percent of its employees into cross-functional teams comprised of IT, networks, products, marketing, and digital people. The agile transformation for the rest of the business—channels, corporate support functions, and other units—began immediately after.

Spark's agile model was built based on a view of where and how value is created in each part of the business. Given the nature of New Zealand's telco sector, Spark decided to place significant focus on "product tribes." These tribes own the customer journey, product management, and related systems for specific products like mobile or IT services, to allow full differentiation and rapid improvement. "Segment tribes" take care of attracting new customers and growing existing ones. Finally, "enabling tribes" provide services and capabilities for other tribes. Channels (such as retail, billing operations, and B2B sales and service) and support functions (such as HR and finance), use a mix of squads, self-managing teams, and other team configurations suited for the nature of the work.

Contrary to what the Spark leadership had been braced to expect from overseas companies that had made the leap to agile, Spark's operating metrics remained rock solid during the transition. Now positive results are flowing in. The new work model with just three "layers" of hierarchy has allowed efficiency through greater focus on productive work. The new 90-day governance cycle—the quarterly business review—allows for more effective and regular steering, higher transparency, and faster decision making across the whole business. Employees are thrilled to work in a setting where they can have direct customer impact, and customers, especially in the B2B space, are starting to notice the difference. In the words of many employees, Spark would "not go back for anything in the world."

Agile implications: 'Open heart surgery while running a marathon'

Each of the operating-model transformations TDC and Spark undertook demonstrates a certain boldness. It's been described as "open-heart surgery while running a marathon"— being prepared to dramatically change a company's core operating model without missing a beat in performance.

Surgeons inform patients of the risks of an operation before performing it, and we want to conclude this article by doing something similar, so you are aware of the implications of embracing agility.

- *The impact on your people is profound.* An agile structure is built around teams of doers with little management overhead. Spark asked about 200 of its top managers to become agile team members, openly acknowledging that agile isn't for everyone. Some chose to leave instead. Also, you need to invest in new skills, such as agile coaching, that previously didn't exist at scale.

- *You must overhaul your core finance and governance processes.* Agile teams need regular direction and prioritization, for which traditional large business cases and multiyear plans that bring comfort to management won't work. TDC leadership needed to get comfortable dealing with 90-day objectives and funding tribes instead of individual projects. This puts more responsibility on leadership to stay on top of details and to work transparently, which can require a mind-set change.

- *The people model and culture need to change.* Valuing and paying people based on hierarchical position won't work in a flat, high-speed organization. Extrinsic motivators like bonuses and job titles need to be reconsidered to enable intrinsic motivation in teams. Culture is so critical to success that nurturing and evolving it will likely take up most of the effort you put into your transformation.

- *The role of the top team is very different.* Agile companies require strongly united leaders to sense the market and shape priorities, but then let the teams figure out how to meet them. At Spark, the top team led the change by becoming a leadership squad and adopting a rhythm of standups, retrospectives, and demos similar to those used by the rest of the business. They centered their deliverables around building a great organization that enables other teams to succeed.

If these realities don't scare you, the best way to start the journey is to build strong alignment and a joint aspiration in your top team. We have found visiting agile companies an enriching and sobering way to start a journey toward agile—hearing the experiences of fellow management teams bypasses theoretical discussion to create a joint understanding of what agile can do for your company. Learn what you want and don't want from an agile model. Then set explicit targets and design principles to keep you honest on what you are trying to achieve. Taking a decisive approach and basing it on the learnings from companies like TDC and Spark will give you the best chance at success.

What matters in customer-experience transformations

McKinsey leaders provide an overview of the A, B, Cs of pulling together the building blocks of a customer-experience transformation.

Few debate the importance of customer experience, but companies still have trouble transforming their organizations to capture all the advantages of excellent customer experience. While approaches vary based on the maturity of the business and the customer opportunities, the most-successful companies address three building blocks: aligning on a strong aspiration, implementing a disciplined process for transformation, and building up the enablers to make it all work (exhibit).

The building blocks of a customer-experience transformation

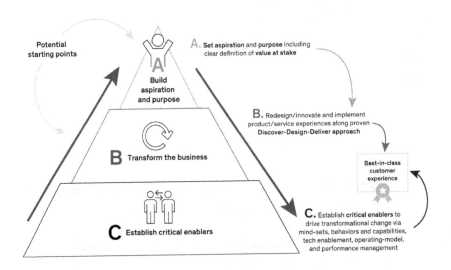

Of course, a simple framework doesn't mean that the transformation isn't complex. Any transformation effort requires leadership, focus, investment, and commitment. But we've found that when companies have a clear view of the building blocks and reference them throughout the transformation journey, they make better decisions and coordinate activities more efficiently.

The remainder of this article provides our leaders' views on approaching customer-experience transformation, accompanied by videos that lay out the most important points.

A holistic approach to customer-experience transformation

A true customer-centric transformation often entails rethinking a business or even the business model itself, which is the only way the transformation can achieve its full impact and remain sustainable. A fundamental change of mind-set focusing on the customer, along with operational and IT improvements, can generate a 20 to 30 percent uplift in customer satisfaction, a 10 to 20 percent improvement in employee satisfaction, and economic gains ranging from 20 to 50 percent of the cost base addressed in the various journeys. In the words of senior partner Harald Fanderl, "There is no silver bullet—only a holistic approach will succeed." That holistic approach relies heavily on all three building blocks. (Building blocks A, B, C.)

Customer-experience transformation: Three major components

Any successful customer-experience program must contain several components. Partner Nicolas Maechler explains: "The first is top-management buy-in on a customer-centric strategy to ensure a shared vision. Secondly, core customer journeys must be identified and transformed by redesigning and digitizing them. Finally, enable the transformation by establishing a permanent, live feedback loop from customers to as many employees as possible." (Building blocks A, B, C.)

The starting point for a transformation

As partner Fransje van der Marel explains, "Customer experience is an excellent starting point for a digital transformation because it places the emphasis on creating a happy customer and will also solve a lot of inherent inefficiencies." Keys to success include engaging with your customer early and throughout the process and employing cross-functional teams to tap into the organization's experiences and expertise. A focus on value and bottom-line value delivery is also critical, as is the ability to create broad excitement within the organization. (Building block C.)

A design perspective

Designing new experiences helps employees connect with the value they are creating for customers, brings cross-functional teams together, and serves as a shared language that allows different departments to communicate more easily. "Designers can use role playing and physical prototypes to see what the experience feels like for the customers and to rapidly test new ideas," says senior partner Stefan Moritz. "Future customer experiences can also be designed to create a "North Star" to guide the organization on its goals-based journey." (Building block B.)

Common themes in customer-experience transformations

In the words of senior partner Tjark Freundt, "Effective customer-experience transformations require a clear vision and a customer-centric, ambitious articulation of goals." Metrics are crucial for understanding customer needs and performance levels, but leaders also need to take a holistic view of the end-to-end customer experience. A typical transformation can take two to three years and relies on attracting or upskilling talent to sustain the continuous improvement necessary for success. (Building blocks A, C.)

Customer-experience measurement; 3 questions, 3 answers

"A customer-experience measurement system typically resides at the core of a transformation," explains Ralph Breuer. "It translates sometimes confusing data to explain what's driving customer satisfaction and shows how to increase it on a daily basis." A customer-experience measurement system links business impact (increased revenue, cost savings) to all the elements that drive customer-satisfaction improvements. A successful measurement system is journey-based, should involve a substantial part of the organization, and can't be cobbled together from existing systems and outdated mind-sets. (Building block C.)

The three building blocks of this framework can help distill the complex challenge of customer-experience transformation, facilitating the journey and in turn improving decision making and coordination.

Instilling a company-wide growth mind-set to achieve both short- and long-term growth

Growth for Scout24 requires a "three-sided" view of the customer.

In this interview, McKinsey's Dennis Spillecke talks to Scout24's chief product and marketing officer, Dr. Thomas Schroeter, about instilling a growth mind-set across the entire workforce. Scout24 is a leading operator of digital marketplaces for real estate and automobiles in Europe, with revenues of more than €500 million in 2018.

How do you empower your workforce with a growth mind-set?

An essential element that we are trying to bring into the company is a growth mind-set. We want to recruit and develop people not on the capability side but on the mental side, starting with this growth mind-set and having high ambitions. We are a strongly growing company and doing well, but we still want to disrupt, and that starts with having the right mind-set. If you have the right mind-set and you combine it with the right strategy and the right operating model, it actually starts flowing.

We've started an internal communication theme called Team 15 to help instill the growth mind-set in the company. It is basically a guerilla exercise. The message is very simple, focused, and articulate: we are one team, and we are trying to grow 15 percent or more. And this growth mind-set is starting to pay off.

How do you think about customer focus?

First, one of the interesting elements at Scout is that we are operating a three-sided marketplace. That means we have the consumer who's looking for, for example, a car or real estate; we have the owner who's selling a car or real estate; and then we have a third party, the real estate agent or the developer or the OEM or the dealer, who also plays a role. So it's a three-sided marketplace that we have to balance.

Second, changing consumer behavior drives change in our business models. We put the consumer first. And if we provide a great experience for the consumer when buying a home or finding a car, or obtaining financing around it, we also have the opportunity to connect the ecosystem. So we try to find the right business model for changing consumer needs but in the context of having a three-sided marketplace, because a marketplace never works with just one party in it.

How do you communicate the growth agenda?

We've introduced objectives and key results (OKRs) on a company-wide level to align and focus the organization and invest in the right capabilities, capacities, and initiatives. We've defined four clear objectives. Then we've broken those down on the different vertical levels: ImmoScout, AutoScout, and consumer services. And then we've broken those down on a market-segment, or business-unit, level. This rolls up in a pyramid, so that if residential real estate at ImmoScout is doing something, it somehow has to contribute to what we are trying to achieve at Scout.

Then, within the OKR framework, we've tried to balance short- and long-term growth. We've been very explicit in that we want to meet and exceed market expectations; that is short-term growth. We also want to build the network marketplace; that is long-term growth. And we have been very specific about how we measure success around the three elements of the network marketplace.

Focusing on culture to drive growth

Embracing a growth mind-set and working with customers to develop innovative new products has been the recipe for growth at Amcor.

In this interview, McKinsey's Biljana Cvetanovski talks to Luca Zerbini, vice president and general manager of Amcor Flexibles EMEA. Amcor is a global packaging company with revenues of $13 billion. The following is an edited version of their conversation.

What are the key ingredients needed for growth?

You need to have an organization that enables you to make growth happen. I would definitely not underestimate the challenge of changing the culture to make that happen. The mind-sets of people are probably the biggest component. We always quote Peter Drucker: "Culture eats strategy for breakfast." It's absolutely true. It took us longer than we thought to change the mind-sets of people. In some cases, we had to change the people that we had in order to make it happen.

I think by now people really live and breathe growth, but in the past, there was much more skepticism: "Why would I change? What's in it for me?" To change this, you need an incentive system and organizational setup that is aligned to growth. And then the communication and the tone from the top has to be consistent in terms of driving customer centricity, organic growth, and collaboration among the different functions, rather than keeping the status quo and just continuing to do what we were doing before.

How do you think about innovation at Amcor?

Amcor is well known in the market for being a very strong innovator. One of the key pieces of feedback we get from our customers is that we have a strong innovation capability. In the past, however, customers would come to us with an issue, and we would say, "OK, we can solve it." We would then create an R&D project and deliver the solution. Very often what would happen, though, was that we would do the same project 200 times because different customers would come to us with different but very similar types of issues. We called that "customer-backed innovation."

What we do now, with the advantage of having done work on the marketing side, is to drive what we call "segment-driven innovation," in which we proactively go to customers and say, "In your specific vertical, in your specific segment, in your specific category, what is important? If you're a coffee customer, what is important in terms of single serve, in terms of roast and ground, in terms of instant soluble? What type of sustainability or consumer requirements do you have? We can help you with this from a packaging perspective." Together with our customers we build an innovation road map that becomes a joint commitment to bring products to market. We do this both with the global key accounts and also regional accounts.

What is the Amcor Growth Opportunity Program?

The Amcor Growth Opportunity Program is about being fast and focused. We want to analyze and understand the market. We want to be clear in segmenting the market and in having a team that is able to drive the execution—and then repeat the process on a consistent basis.

It's about how you understand the market and your competition, and then quantify that and make sure you understand the needs of customers. It is about how you listen to them, structure their needs, segment the market, define a unique selling proposition to respond to the needs or pain points of the market, and then have an execution plan that addresses all the obstacles or opportunities for growth. The execution plan becomes something that is driven by the same team that has driven the analysis of the categories, so people are excited about crafting the future and then making it happen.

Focusing on customers and team mind-sets to deliver growth

The key to achieving sustainable growth at Danone is a strategy focused on what customers want and building up a growth mind-set within the business.

In this interview, McKinsey's Eric Hazan talks to Danone's Francisco Camacho, Executive Vice President of Essential Dairy and Plant-Based, about fostering a growth mind-set. Danone is a French multinational food-products corporation based in Paris, with revenues of almost €25 billion in 2018. The following is an edited version of the interview.

How do you think about growth strategy?

In any given business, it always starts with strategy. Every time I come to a business, I take a look at it, no matter if it is big or small or medium, and then develop a clear set of strategies. That set of strategies will be focused on where you want to take the business. So you say, "I want to take the business to that place." What are the strategies to reach that place or that objective?"

Any business will require very strong innovation, it will require very strong execution in the marketplace, and then, depending on the type of business, it's likely that you will also consider geographic expansion or portfolio expansion, or other actions.

What are the challenges to growth?

That balance of short, mid, and long-term is always very delicate, and if you break it, then it takes a lot of effort to fix it and to put it back so that there's a positive momentum. If the balance is not the right one, then you put the business in jeopardy.

There are other growth challenges when there is a difficult economy context. When the economic situation in a country is not good, it is always more challenging. And there is also the aspect of how the teams are behaving within that difficult context.

Another challenge to sustaining growth is when you have lost touch with your consumers or with what consumers want. In the type of businesses we're in, it is always key to keep the consumer at the center of our decisions, at the center of what we do. It sounds like a cliché, but unfortunately it is often forgotten, and there are many other things that get in the way. We try to put things out there that are convenient for financial reasons, efficiency reasons, or manufacturing reasons, and many other reasons that we have as companies, and every now and then that means that we're forgetting what consumers need and want. That also creates a challenging situation when it comes to growth. Keeping consumers very close, knowing exactly what they want, and giving it to them are key for a good sustainable growth strategy.

How do you assess a team's growth mindset?

When I talk to teams, one of the first things that I try to understand is how they are feeling about their growth prospects. If someone comes to me and says, "We're growing in line with the market or slightly above, and we're getting share, and I feel comfortable with that," but I know that the market share they have is not yet at the levels we could achieve, then I will always think that they are not necessarily being as aggressive in terms of growth potential as they could be, because there is always an additional growth lever that you could tap into to get more growth.

If, on the other hand, you have a market in which they already have a high penetration, very high market share, and they are constantly growing ahead of the market, then that's a different thing, and you have to deal with that differently. So my approach is you always need to assess where the teams are in terms of their mentality regarding growth. If they are already thinking that it's so difficult that they cannot do better than they have done historically, then you need to intervene and give them a better perspective in terms of what the possibilities are.

How do you implement the growth mind-set?

While I'd rather have stable growth than no growth at all, if you really want to reach the true potential of a business, you have to be leaping in terms of growth. The growth mentality is easier to achieve when individuals or the leaders of the organization have been exposed to situations in which a lot of things are thrown at them and they have had to adapt and to move fast and to do things that were not done in the past.

That's the type of mentality that I try to get our teams to have, which is don't think that a normal situation has to stay "normal" to deliver growth. It's actually better if the situation is a bit different and you are constantly not happy with what you are achieving, so that you always strive to achieve a little bit more in terms of growth. That's what I mean about mentality. When I look at what people do in markets in which the volatility is high—and anything can happen in any given year—the mind-set changes. And when you then put these types of people into a more stable market, it will be easier for them to challenge the norm.

How purpose-driven growth and a strong culture can beat the market

The foundation of growth strategy at Mondelēz is built on focusing the company, from leadership to the front lines, on a shared purpose.

M cKinsey's Dennis Spillecke talks growth with Mondelēz International's chief marketing officer for Europe, Debora Koyama. Mondelēz is a multinational confectionary and food and beverage company, with revenues of £20 billion. The following is an edited version of their conversation.

How do you think about purpose-driven growth?

We have a new purpose at Mondelēz, which is to empower people to snack right. People really relate to that. Our employees are excited about it, and I think that's critical, as we're trying to really go after growth. Then there is a purpose that we can really unlock through our portfolio of brands. I believe in purpose delivering growth. I've seen it in my career, and we have so many hard data and facts showing that purpose drives growth. Why purpose? For me, humans need it. I think everybody needs purpose and meaning in their lives. I think employees thrive on it, society expects it from us in business, and finally, if nothing else, purpose delivers growth.

How are you developing the company's growth culture?

We have a new set of leadership values, behaviors, and commitments that I'm very excited about. One is reigniting the values, commitments, and behaviors related to loving consumers and brands. The other one is thinking about growth every day. One of the commitments is having a growth mind-set. To me, this is a critical one. I think it is instrumental to success today to have the beginner's mind-set, to be able and willing to learn every day, especially in this fast-paced digital world that's changing every hour. That's a very exciting and critical factor in shifting the culture as we go into the new phase.

What does it mean to grow in a digital age?

I think this is one of the most exciting times to be in marketing, or in brands, because we have so many ways to connect with consumers. We have never had so many ways to have a conversation with people. So that's number one. Two, with data we are able also to have a much more personalized conversation with groups of people. We talk a lot about personalization at scale. The third one is the data we have to support and make marketing much more precise through the consumer decision journey.

A passion for customer experience in driving growth

Embracing data and providing an enhanced customer experience have been keys to growth at Hugo Boss.

In this interview, McKinsey's Dennis Spillecke talks to Linda Dauriz, director of customer experience and corporate development at Hugo Boss, about data-driven growth and customer experience. Hugo Boss is a luxury fashion company with revenues of $3 billion. The following is an edited version of the highlights of the interview.

What are your recommendations for a leader looking to spark growth?

For fueling growth, I have three recommendations. The first one is to be very clear about your priorities, so you know what you want your team to go after. Be extremely clear why you want them to go after that opportunity and why you believe it's exactly the right path for the organization.

The second is to hire for a growth mind-set. Seek people who are living a can-do mentality and enjoy challenges but who also see the opportunities that arise from challenges.

The third and last one is to show your personal passion for the growth area you're pursuing, because a certain energy level and being passionate about growth definitely have a positive impact on everyone around you.

How are you enhancing customer experience to drive growth?

It all started with a provocative statement, that "experiences will be the new product." I definitely shocked quite a few in a very product-oriented company when I made this statement. It all starts with the brand and what the brand embodies. Boss dresses the drive of our customers, so we are there on their journey—on their personal journey to growth and to success. For us, the core was this notion of ambition and drive, and we built experiences around that.

One format, for example, is an evening in our store, combining career and styling advice, that we titled "Live Up to Your Ambition." This is really buying a piece of the Boss world, and we're testing whether customers are willing to spend their money not on the next suit but on an evening that will lead them to live up to their ambition.

What is the role of data in growth?

Three years ago, we took the decision to insource our customer database, and since then we have been obsessed with customer data. The first step is in the stores: we encourage all of our staff and employees, through competitions, to register our customers so that we know who is coming through the door and who is buying our brand.

Having captured customer data, then we leverage analytical models to truly understand our customer behavior in depth. What we realized is that our colleagues in sales get more and more enthusiastic about the power of data. They were rather skeptical in the beginning, but then when you explain to them that we can predict with a high chance what the next buy will be, or when they will be next in store, that excites them and also motivates them to register more and more customers.

We were able to massively increase the share of net sales through registered members.

The role of customer care in a customer experience transformation

No function handles a broader range of customer touchpoints than customer care. Executives would be wise to make it the centerpiece of any effort to transform the customer experience.

C **onsumer expectations are rising** across the board—not due to a specific industry but from all of the excellent interactions that leading companies provide. Executives have recognized that customer satisfaction is the key indicator in gauging success, but too often a focus on specific touchpoints or channels results in incremental progress that only allows a company to keep pace with the changing customer landscape. Leading executives have recognized that really moving the needle on customer satisfaction requires a more ambitious effort—a transformation of the entire customer experience.

Gaining a comprehensive view of the customer journey is easier said than done, and initiatives that attempt to adopt a customer-centric mind-set can fall short without both a clear top-line strategy and a granular view of customer behavior. Even as technology and data from engagement channels provide companies with increased visibility into customer touchpoints, weaving all of this information together into a clear and coherent picture of the customer can be a formidable challenge. The complexity of customer interactions in multiple channels, for example, means that information resides throughout the enterprise—in not only customer care but also marketing, sales, product development, and back-office functions.

Designing excellent customer journeys—an orchestrated sequence of touchpoints that customers traverse to address common requests and issues, often in a mix of live and digital channels—is critical to a customer-experience transformation. This process of mapping customer journeys is the only way to truly get a comprehensive view of the entire gamut of touchpoints and how they fit together. Customer care, which typically includes the call center as well as online and self-service channels, has an integral role to play. As the natural owner of a large part of the customer journey, customer care can provide invaluable insight by helping to define journeys, identify pain points, and spur collaboration across functions. Such actions can produce additional benefits: an end-to-end redesign of the customer journey can not only transform the customer experience but also reduce operating costs in customer care.

Why the customer journey matters in a customer-experience transformation

Traditionally, efforts to enhance customer experience have focused on gathering a tremendous amount of detail about individual touchpoints—identifying the key moments that have an outsize impact on customer satisfaction, determining why care fell short, and developing remedies to improve service. Leaders of different functions such as sales, marketing, and customer care would devote significant time and resources to optimizing interactions within the channels they managed—but a lack of visibility across functions hindered more sweeping, lasting progress.

Organizations that can break out of this siloed mentality have the potential to gain an unprecedented view of the customer. The digitization of the entire customer journey, including the use of digital channels and self-service tools, is well under way. And leading organizations are using increasing volumes of data to link the customer journey and customer satisfaction to overall strategy and top-line metrics on growth and operational performance (Exhibit 1). By understanding how operational factors such as speed and first-call resolution translate into customer satisfaction, contact centers can ensure they focus their energy and resources on areas that have the greatest impact on the customer experience. When these efforts are aligned with the organization's overall goals, this enhanced experience contributes to a higher recommendation rate—a core metric for the company.

Exhibit 1

The pyramid model links customer satisfaction to business outcomes.

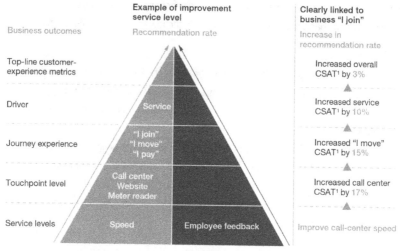

	Example of improvement service level	Clearly linked to business "I join"
Business outcomes	Recommendation rate	Increase in recommendation rate
Top-line customer-experience metrics		Increased overall CSAT¹ by 3%
Driver	Service	Increased service CSAT¹ by 10%
Journey experience	"I join" "I move" "I pay"	Increased "I move" CSAT¹ by 15%
Touchpoint level	Call center Website Meter reader	Increased call center CSAT¹ by 17%
Service levels	Speed	Employee feedback	Improve call-center speed

¹Customer satisfaction.

Customer care's vital role in the transformation

For more and more organizations, customer care is playing an essential and natural role in mapping the customer journey, but to do so the function must often overcome several barriers. The function began as the call center, which was responsible for just one touchpoint and largely transactional. In an omnichannel world, customer care is increasingly becoming a major contributor to customer satisfaction across a broad range of customer channels, from chat and social media to service apps and self-service channels. In some organizations the function is still perceived as executional rather than strategic, focused primarily on handling low-value requests. In addition, the proliferation of channels and touchpoints over the years has increased the number of entities within the enterprise that engage with customers. So while customer care remained at the center of customer experience, functions such as sales and marketing were viewed as having a better understanding of customers. Last, obstacles to information sharing and collaboration sometimes muted customer care's influence on shaping customer-experience strategies. In less-advanced organizations, for example, even basic tasks such as making changes to the website hosted in the marketing department can prove a challenge.

The truth is that customer care should be closely involved in designing customer journeys: the function encompasses all touchpoints and organizational units with a clear service component, such as branches, field service, and contact centers that handle calls, emails, chats, and back-office tasks. The organizational setup of customer care reflects this reach. Many organizations have an integrated approach that bundles responsibility for the different channels into one unit, and the rise of omnichannel has accelerated this development. Thanks to customer care's responsibilities, its frontline agents enable the function to hear the "voice of the customer" on a daily basis, monitor trends and overall sentiment, and identify pain points, improvement levers, and success factors.

One major European telco, for example, recently redesigned its customer service organization, reorienting it from separate functions bound by common technology platforms to an entity focused on segments defined by different customer journeys. In this reorganization, customer care assumed responsibility for not only the contact center but also all service-relevant processes (including field services), enabling it to manage the end-to-end customer experience for the majority of service journeys.

Customer care's role and responsibilities give it the ability to advance the customer transformation in several ways:

1. *Own customer journeys.* Customer care controls a significant number of touchpoints across primary channels, making it the natural owner of many service-focused customer journeys. With insights from these customer interactions, customer care is also in a unique position to inform the strategy of sales, marketing, and product development, among other functions.

2. *Implement improvement measures.* When issues arise, customer care's position enables it to take action to improve customer experience—either for one specific journey or across common touchpoints in all journeys. The function is often the first to

detect operational and product issues: for example, one retailer's customer-care function identified a pattern of unreliable parcel delivery first and brought the issue to the logistics department's attention.

3. *Catalyze performance improvement.* Customer care can assemble a detailed picture of the overall experience through the customer's eyes (Exhibit 2). With this perspective, it can identify the different touchpoints and channels in a given journey as well as the departments or functions that own the interaction.

Exhibit 2

In an omnichannel approach, all formats are essential to the customer journey.

○ Potential to use channel in an omnichannel setup   ● Most commonly used channels for task

Channel

Typical steps in an "I join" journey (when signing a contract)	Marketing	Mail	Home page, FAQs[1]	Portal	Social media	Email	Fax	App	Branch office	Telephone	Video confer-ence	Chat	Text message	Sales agent
"I inform myself"	●	○	●	○	●	○	○	○	○	○	○	○	○	●
"I declare my interest and ask for information"	○	●	●	○	○	●	○	○	●	●	●	●	○	●
"I fill in my contract (and need help)"	○	●	●	○	○	○	○	○	○	●	●	●	○	●
"I receive my contract confirmation and supporting material"	○	●	○	○	○	●	○	○	○	○	○	○	○	○
"I log in to the portal"	○	○	○	●	○	○	○	○	○	○	○	○	○	○

[1] Frequently asked questions.

Cross-functional collaboration in customer journeys

The complexity of customer journeys, in which a customer can leap from touchpoint to touchpoint across channels, highlights the need for cross-functional collaboration. The following "I join" sample journey, which depicts the path an individual takes from initial interest to conversion, specifies the customer interaction and functional ownership at each step.

- *I inform myself.* The initial contact by a customer to learn more about a company's products and services is usually the responsibility of marketing and sales.

- *I declare my interest and ask for information.* This step is often handled by a specific sales channel such as a branch office. However, customer care frequently discovers sales opportunities as part of customer service

- *I fill in my contract (and need help).* The contact center typically fields these requests, which consist of straightforward administrative issues in the onboarding process. By filling in the gaps of the online journey, customer care can be a partner when questions arise or problems occur.

- *I receive my contract information.* Customer contact is often triggered by a sales-specific, back-office process such as autopay details. These requests can also be handled by a contact center.

- *I log in to the portal.* While a separate department (often marketing) may manage online portals, in an omnichannel world responsibility for the online portal can fall under the purview of customer care. Notably, if the online portal isn't initially presented as part of the product or service, customers could overlook this channel, leading companies to miss out on engagement opportunities.

This exercise is essential to ensure that each function has visibility into the handoffs in a customer journey and that their internal processes are aligned with each channel. Every industry stands to benefit from gaining greater insight into common customer journeys. For example, several service industries, such as insurance, banking, utilities, and telcos, have similar "I join" and "I quit" journeys. Almost all industries have an "I complain" journey. Other journeys are industry-specific: for example, utilities might realize that when a customer moves, it represents a moment of truth. Customers do not usually perceive their utility company as very visible; often they do not even know which contract they are subscribed in.

Since moving houses is one of the very few moments when customers actively engage with the utility, "I move" is therefore an important journey. Similarly, in insurance, "I have a claim" can represent a moment of truth where effective customer service is critical.

Adapting operations to enhance customer experience

Customer care's ownership of such a broad range of customer touchpoints makes it a vital part of understanding and mapping customer journeys. However, the function is well positioned to translate the insights from customer journeys into new ways of working that can improve the customer experience.

Overcome organizational barriers. Aggregating the collective knowledge of leaders from different functions is crucial to assemble a detailed and accurate picture of each customer journey. Even in a customer journey with seemingly well-defined responsibility for service and sales, collaboration can uncover touch points that can naturally be handled by customer-care organizations.

Understand each touchpoint within context. Although every customer journey can consist of multiple touchpoints, determining the next steps requires an awareness of the context—not just the process, but also also the emotions and mindset of customers in which the contact is taking place. Acknowledging a customer's history, even if customer-care leaders are powerless to change it for the better, can improve the experience along the whole journey. At Disney's theme parks, for example, optimizing the customer journey might start prior to entering the park, but service agents should also take into account the emotional context. A family may have taken a long and exhausting trip to get there but may also be excited, and this insight can give agents the necessary context to guide interactions and improve the journey experience.

Identify universal pain points and develop solutions. The "I join" approach can identify pain points within a specific journey, but it can also highlight universal pain points within a given channel. For example, if a company fails to provide a certain level of service, this pain point could apply to all contacts independent of the specific journey. Similarly, optimizing workforce management can improve all touch points in the certain channels. For instance, a more effective contact center can have a direct impact on customer satisfaction (due to lower waiting times) and operating costs (due to higher productivity). In these cases, companies can derive greater value by applying improvements across different journeys.

Achieving a customer-experience transformation requires top-line strategy, but its success ultimately hinges on the outcome of millions of individual touchpoints. Stitching these interactions into a cohesive, granular picture of customer segments is no small task: it requires insights from across the organization. As the front line, customer care should not just have a seat at the table; the function and its managers should be prepared to lead the charge.

Driving toward growth: Making difficult decision and placing the customer first

The key to above-market growth at Aliaxis is a mind-set that keeps the customer first.

Aliaxis is a global leader in the manufacture and distribution of piping. It posted revenues of €3.1 billion in 2018 and has grown at 4 percent over the last four years. Aliaxis executive-committee member Lars Boetje spoke with McKinsey's Biljana Cvetanovski about how the company captures such exceptional results. The following is an edited version of their discussion.

What is your formula for growth?

I think people need to understand that growth is a difficult and tough job. The Aliaxis formula doesn't necessarily work for another company. Each company, each situation, warrants a different formula, so you need to dig in and understand what is required.

For me there are always three growth horizons: it's about tomorrow, next month, and next year. For Aliaxis, it was more important first to start on delivering growth, to focus on tangible initiatives by going where the growth is, and on sales-force excellence. Then, once we were in the journey and had proven some of the capabilities we wanted to deliver , we could rebrand. But we could rebrand only when we had something to back that up. If we'd started the rebranding with nothing there, it would have been an empty proposition for the customer

How do you think about organic growth at Aliaxis?

For me, there are three elements of organic growth. The first one, which doesn't apply only to big businesses, is to go where the growth can be found. We decided to invest in India because it's a growing market, so it has a tailwind. A tailwind is always easier than headwind. You can even outgrow that market. The second element is growing existing businesses, which is built more around commercial actions. That's also the need to go where the growth is, but on a more granular level. Then the third element, very specific for Aliaxis, is that we're one of the few global companies in our space. We have therefore defined growth platforms on a global basis where there is a preferential chance for growth, and also a certain customer need. A good example is high-rise buildings. Obviously, through urbanization, there is much more demand for high-rise buildings, but their piping systems are also much more complex, with different requirements.

What is the key to a growth leadership mind-set?

I think the core of the growth leadership mind-set is placing the customer first in your mind. If you understand what the customer wants and needs, then in the end you can grow. This requires the leadership team to also understand what the key problems are for the customer. This is not always easy, because you're far away and removed from the customer, yet you need to understand so you can also empower the rest of the organization, especially the sales or marketing organization, to make the right choices in order to grow.

Personally, I myself joined a plumber for a day, following him from early morning from his doorstep to the end of the day when he came home. I think that gave me so much insight in terms of what he wanted, what he needed, what he feared, and what we could therefore do as

The importance of innovation and purpose in capturing growth

At British telco giffgaff, growth comes from a formula for making the best decisions.

I n this interview, McKinsey's Biljana Cvetanovski discusses the role of innovation and how to think about growth capabilities with Ashley Schofield, CEO of giffgaff, a telecommunications company headquartered in London, with revenues of $500 million. The following is an edited version of their conversation.

How do you think about the innovation pipeline and ideation?

I think the number-one thing to identify is that ideas can come from anywhere. Often it's our really smart people in data science and business intelligence flagging a trend or finding that we need to act on one. But people can also have a moment of inspiration while traveling on the tube or riding in on a scooter. It's about trying to create a repository, if you like, for those ideas. We have a massive whiteboard in marketing where people are invited to write up an idea regardless of where it's come from or who they are in the business. We also have an ideation platform within our online community for our member base, so they're constantly giving us new ideas and voting on ideas, so the best ones rise to the top. Another thing that I think you need to challenge yourself on, in today's world in particular, is to not start with the solution. Instead, start with the problem and be really clear what the problem is before you start chucking in solutions.

Is there a formula or methodology you use for growth?

We do have a formula for decisions we make around growth. We call it the giffgaff artichoke. In it are the kind of ingredients that make great decisions for giffgaff. One box starts with, is it consistent with our values and sense of purpose? If it isn't, then that's a deal breaker; we won't go there. Secondly, is it exciting? Is there a sense that, if we arrive there, we could generate a sense of infectious purpose about it? If the answers to the first two questions are yes, then we also look for the mutuality piece: Is there a give-and-get element with our membership that would help the dynamic work? Then the fourth bit: Is it scalable? There are lots of things that we could do, but ultimately we're interested in impact. So we want to do things that will impact on a sizable scale. Those are the four ingredients that keep us honest on making those tough decisions.

What capabilities have been critical for delivering growth at giffgaff?

To thrive at giffgaff you need to be comfortable with empowerment; it's not the kind of place where people are going to tell you what to do. What they will do instead is frame things for you and say, "We think the answer might lie over there; here are some resources; let us know how you get on." Some people will thrive in that environment, but others will find it challenging.

Secondly, I think a question to ask from a resources point of view is: What is the real work to be done here? I think there are two critical business choices we've made at giffgaff that have propelled our growth forward. One is that five years ago, we brought management of the brand in house and parted ways with marketing agencies because we felt like we had a better understanding of who we were than anybody else. We wanted to drive how that was shared with the rest of the world, so we brought it in house. I'm not aware of any other telco that does that.

We approached things similarly with technology. Technology is the element that brings experiences to life for our members. So why on earth would we outsource that to anyone else? We wanted that in house, colocated with the marketing folks and everyone else in the business so we could continue to connect with our audience and do the right thing. For us, owning that brand story and identity, and finding smart ways to deliver great tech, great experiences—those are the skill sets that we really value.

What do you see as the future of marketing?

The way I like to think of it now is that what you really need to create is a marketing-technology love child. That's the sweet spot, because the people who write the code, who deliver the experiences, really need to have that marketing orientation. Otherwise, there's a disconnect. Getting marketing and technology closer together is therefore what we're pursuing at the moment, creating teams that have both of those skill sets and really value. Then, delivering that to our membership on a daily basis so we're getting some feedback from them. We've got the skills from a marketing perspective to dig in beyond the obvious and then be able to act on it.

Zero-based productivity—Marketing: Measure, allocate, and invest marketing dollars more effectively

Taking a zero-based budgeting approach to enterprise-wide marketing costs can uncover new opportunities and spur more-informed spending decisions.

Marketing is critical to growth and consumer engagement, and its costs can account for more than 10 percent of revenues in many consumer-facing businesses. Yet few companies have fundamentally changed how they measure and assess marketing's impact—often resulting in budgets and programs that are close cousins of years past. And few marketers are confident about identifying the real return on investment (ROI) of their marketing spending, or the impact of trade-offs.

This apparent paradox derives from a time when the bulk of the marketing budget was concentrated in above-the-line channels such as TV and radio, which are characterized by more limited measurability of outcomes than are typical of below-the-line activities such as search-engine marketing. And, since most companies build budgets based on the previous year's spending levels, it has taken a long time for deep discussions of marketing ROI to reach the boardroom and become an executive-level priority.

In recent years, the proliferation of technologies that can process massive data sets, combined with the growth of digital advertising channels—which are inherently more measurable—has unlocked a massive opportunity to measure the performance of marketing investments. Even though analytical tools have become more widely available, our experience suggests that few companies apply the same level of scrutiny to overall spending in marketing categories. In fact, more than 60 percent of Fortune 1000 chief marketing officers claim that they cannot quantify the impact of marketing in both the short and long term.

To gain a more detailed view of marketing and sales expenditures, organizations must overcome several barriers. First, marketing budgets are often separate for each business unit and country, which limits visibility and comparisons. Second, the multitude of spending categories can make it difficult to identify the highest-value opportunities. Last, companies tend to use media agencies to manage, or at least intermediate, a significant share of their marketing spending—and agencies are often more interested in maintaining historical spending levels and allocations than challenging past assumptions to achieve savings. All of these challenges are underpinned by an entrenched, reactive mind-set when it comes to setting priorities and budgets.

These very obstacles, however, also make marketing and sales spending categories especially ripe for cost savings. Zero-based marketing—a comprehensive approach that extends zero-based budgeting principles to marketing categories across the enterprise— can uncover opportunities for savings worth 10 to 25 percent of spending in certain categories, and these funds can be reallocated to higher-value areas. In fact, with the rare exception of industries that are in a global state of decline, a well-executed reinvestment in high-ROI opportunities will deliver a greater return than "banking the savings" will. A recent McKinsey survey revealed businesses that are methodical about investing funds unlocked through zero-based budgeting and other programs into growth—either proven winners or future products and services—outperform the market. Notably, often more than 50 percent of these savings can be achieved in the first 12 months of a zero-based marketing effort, allowing for a very rapid reallocation.

Gaining a granular view of spending and opportunities

Zero-based marketing requires commercial leaders to pause and ask five critical questions.

1. Based on bottom-up analyses, what are realistic but ambitious targets for our company?

Companies need clarity about the fundamental drivers of their value creation, but often the drivers are not consistently understood or thoroughly applied when the strategy is developed. Business value is created by improving return on invested capital or top-line growth (for example, increased market share, positive market momentum, or a combination of both). Hence it is crucial to set targets that are consistent with the life stage of each area of the business in relation to consumer demand and preferences. These targets need to be defined through bottom-up analysis of revenue pools and growth drivers.

For example, the leadership team at a fast-moving consumer goods company could consider reallocating marketing dollars from products in its portfolio that have sizable market share in a low-growth category to products with the potential to gain share in high-growth categories. Although this action sounds intuitive, companies with cost-plus budgeting often don't have a culture that enables conversations about such resource allocation.

Zero-based marketing establishes the lines of communication across business units and functions as well as the cadence for growth discussions. These efforts help to avoid underfunding areas with limited potential and instead free up resources to invest in high-ROI opportunities that might be overlooked or left with the crumbs after the demands of historically larger business areas have been satisfied.

2. How do we understand what is driving marketing costs?

The many marketing spending categories that exist are driven by different factors. To thoughtfully reduce, reallocate, or increase marketing spending across various categories, it is essential to establish a baseline where every dollar can be linked to a driver (or set of drivers) that determines why that money is being spent.

For instance, we can separate media spending into two categories: working and nonworking. The former is shaped by the reach, frequency, and quality of the advertisement the company deploys to communicate with customers; the latter is determined by the amount of creative, production, and research activity performed to create assets such as a TV ad, and it is not directly driven by how many customers will see or react to the asset. Therefore, the logic by which each of these media spending categories will be assessed is very different. In most cases, this approach would go one or two levels deeper to identify much more granular factors. For working media, examples are the number of customers acquired (or retained) during the ad airing period and the recall rate of the ad among target customers; for nonworking media, factors could be the reuse rate of existing ads and creative assets and the average production cost per asset, among others.

Establishing a common currency, where every dollar spent can be compared against others and decisions can be linked back to objective drivers, is fundamental to zero-based marketing.

3. How can the organization establish the right conversations to identify opportunities?

Marketing leaders have to work very closely with finance and other functions on resource allocation decisions. As mentioned before, marketing teams should set clear targets for growth and market share based on value-creation potential.

Then, rather than trying to understand the absolute spending on TV campaigns, for example, teams should compare saturation levels and gross rating points (GRPs) per message to find opportunities. Instead of oversaturating a target group, funds could be redirected to a campaign highlighting new products or brands. Similarly, in digital channels such as social media, data should be presented to quantify the impact on awareness, consideration, and conversion, not just presence or share of voice. In this way, the discussions become more structured and fact-based, allowing changes in direction to be clearly supported and communicated—while also aligning marketing spending more tightly with strategic priorities.

4. How can an organization reallocate funds among the different cost types to ensure it is maximizing ROI?

Commercial leaders very often have all the data they need to assess the relative productivity of various spending categories and their coherence with consumer needs and competitors' positioning. Zero-based marketing compels managers to rely on factual information to achieve consensus. With data-driven insights, generic statements such as "We should spend more in digital" or "We should continue to invest most of our money in Brand A because it's our power brand" either become more meaningful or are exposed as myths.

Companies can then make better spending decisions—for example, by allocating less to above-the-line campaigns and more to personalized communications through digital channels or customer-relationship-management (CRM) campaigns. In some situations, the ROI from a secondary in-store display might be greater than that of a price promotion. Such information provides commercial leaders with the tools to shift their spending.

5. What is the best way to track funds freed up in other areas to enable growth?

A zero-based approach establishes a consistent terminology for spending and investment, making ROI and budget discipline the common ground for decision making. At a global manufacturing company, for example, the CEO used the same cost-management tool that had been tracking budgets and spending for zero-based budgeting to plan, track, and monitor growth initiatives. The change resulted in more transparent budgeting decisions about which initiatives to finance and an ability to track and redirect resources during the course of the year to ensure optimal spending. The company achieved the target ROI.

More important than the tools and methodology used, however, is personal commitment on the part of marketing leaders. In all zero-based marketing efforts, commercial executives must provide marketing managers with full ownership of their respective cost areas, along with targets to achieve in the form of ROI, and where relevant, savings and reinvestment.

Establishing a governance mechanism to track progress of these owners against their commitments is a fundamental step to ensuring that growth targets are met as a result of the adoption of zero-based marketing.

Impact of zero-based marketing

One EU-based consumer packaged-goods company launched a zero-based marketing program with the goal of redirecting funds from marketing and sales categories to support of new growth initiatives. The management team was skeptical of the cost savings it could achieve, since these categories had been scrutinized already.

As a first step, the team created a database of more than 50 spending categories across business units and regions. It then applied industry benchmarks to set targets for each category. Using this detailed information, the team identified cost-savings initiatives, including removing some components from the media agency contract reducing overall agency fees, and cutting packaging design costs. The zero-based approach created new budgets and a proactive cost-management process for each category.

The impact was significant: a 15 percent increase in spending efficiency, with more than 70 percent of the opportunities coming from nonworking media levers. More important, the process helped to instill an ownership mind-set among marketing and sales managers, enabling cost-reduction efforts to be sustained beyond the initial stages.

In another case, an online gaming operator was in a period of stagnating revenue growth while marketing costs—mostly for digital channels—were increasing year on year due to market inflation and increasing competition. With profitability coming under pressure, management was compelled to take a hard look at the cost of acquiring new customers in relation to their value. By mapping all of the marketing activities and their contribution to new customer acquisitions and then linking them to the behavior and economics of the customers acquired, executives were able to rank their spending categories in order of effectiveness.

They were stunned by the results: 15 percent of their marketing was destroying value by bringing in low-value customers at a negative ROI. In the space of three months, marketing leaders cut spending in those areas and used the savings to finance high-potential channels. One such channel was programmatic media buying, a methodology that allows the marketing function to precisely target specific customers using personalized messages and offers based on their behavior. With the savings, the function was also able to build a rich data set comprising third-party sources of data such as social media activity.

It has never been easier for companies to reassess their level of marketing spending, where funds are allocated, and ROI by category. From greater access to data to media agencies with in-house capabilities to measure the performance of marketing activities, companies have a range of tools and support at their disposal. All that remains is for marketing executives to use those tools to embrace a more analytical, granular approach to spending decisions.

Four pathways to digital growth that work for B2B companies

Here's what it takes for industrial companies to outgrow their peers and create sustainable value from digitization at scale.

Digital leaders in B2B achieve up to five times the revenue growth and up to eight times the EBIT (earnings before interest and taxes) growth of their peers (Exhibit 1). But so far, only one in three companies has deployed digital solutions at scale. "I realize that with my analytics transformation, I've been tossing around pebbles, but no rock," the CEO of a global corporation admits.

Exhibit 1

B2B digital leaders significantly outperform their peers.

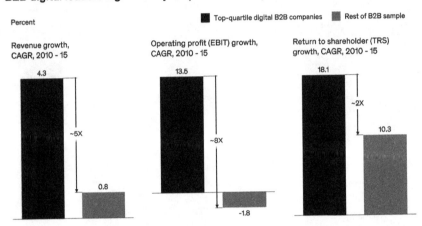

Percent

| | Top-quartile digital B2B companies | Rest of B2B sample |

Revenue growth, CAGR, 2010 - 15

Operating profit (EBIT) growth, CAGR, 2010 - 15

Return to shareholder (TRS) growth, CAGR, 2010 - 15

4.3 ~5X 0.8

13.5 ~8X -1.8

18.1 ~2X 10.3

However, sitting and waiting is not an option. Those who fail to take a shaping posture risk being left behind by the competition or cut out of the value chain entirely. Our analysis of the practices of top performers indicates that the principal challenge is to identify the transformation path (or combination of paths) that suits a given company. Digital leaders in B2B consistently have a clear sense of which pathway holds the biggest potential for their business, and once their mind is made up, they pull out all the stops. They free up cash for investments in data, technology, and talent; they think big, they act fast, and they are prepared to adapt their stance as the market evolves.

Cracking the digital growth code

What does it take to create value from digitization in B2B? To crack the digital growth code, we have examined the practices of top performers. In our 2019 benchmarking study, we have identified four promising transformation pathways, or archetypes, that allow B2B companies to unlock digital growth potential (Exhibit 2):

- *Modernize core commercial processes*, such as sales and pricing, with data and analytics to improve performance

- *Redesign the customer journey*, to make the procurement of industrial supplies, for example, as convenient as shopping on Amazon

- *Disrupt the channel* to expand the margin pool, for example, by establishing a direct web presence and route-to-market to access new customer segments

- *Build tomorrow's unicorns* to secure growth beyond the core business or defend against digital attackers.

Exhibit 2

An overview of the four transformation archetypes highlights their differences.

	A Modernize core commercial processes	**B** Digitize to differentiate experience	**C** Disrupt the channel	**D** Create unicorns
What The focus	Embed analytics into core commercial processes (eg, pricing, sales)	Redesign and digitize customer journeys (eg, online ordering)	Go directly to customers (eg, new platform)	Build and grow new business models of scale
Why The purpose	To upgrade commercial capabilities and drive expansion of margin & sales	To drive strategic differentiation based on experience	To control end-customer relationship and drive growth/margin	To create attractive, new, organic growth
How The approach	Establish commercial analytics center of excellence Deploy use cases to the front line with training	Set up studio/digital factory Create up to 4 cross-functional squads operating sprints (with releases)	"Build on the side" and integrate later Articulate channel strategy and wargame channel conflicts	Introduce in-house incubator Cross-functional squads with business development leadership
Outcomes	+1 to 2% sales +1 to 3% margin	20 → 80% digital interactions +1 to 5 percentage points market share	Ownership of end customer +1 to 3% margin	Business creation at scale Business-model reinvention

To prioritize pathways and identify the capabilities they need to invest in, companies should develop a clear understanding of the current and future economics of the business, asking questions such as:

- Where does the money come from today?

- Where will (or could) it come from in the future?

- What is the degree of digital maturity of core commercial domains, from sales management to pricing and marketing?

Based on the outcome of this exercise, companies can create what is sometimes referred to as the "value map" (Exhibit 3). This will help them focus their resources and their funds on the most promising digital opportunities, instead of rushing down one pathway prematurely. In this context, clarity and consensus about what a company should not do is just as important as the determination to pursue the most promising pathway to digital growth with full force.

Exhibit 3

The effect of value levers can be mapped by domains and business units.

Value potential

		Low	Medium	High

Domain	Commercial levers	Business unit 1				Business unit 2			
		APAC	Europe	NA	Total	APAC	Europe	NA	Total
Sales-growth optimization	Churn								
	Win-back								
	Share-of-wallet								
	Upsell								
	Cross-sell								
	Revenue from white space								
	Sales productivity (cost savings)								
	Sales productivity (FTE savings)								
Pricing and margin management	Transactional pricing								
	Commodity pricing								
	Value pricing								
Business-model innovation	Percentage of revenue from nonproduct sales								
Customer-experience design	Demand forecasting accuracy								
	Sales and operations planning								
	Improved margin from customer experience								
Risk	Risk reduction/hedging								

A company may choose to combine multiple pathways or pursue multiple objectives consecutively. For example, the introduction of a direct channel may be followed by the deployment of advanced analytics to drive commercial excellence across all channels. In the majority of successful cases we have seen, companies start digitizing core processes before they experiment with new business models.

What follows is an overview of the pathways, case examples of how a company pursued each approach, and key success factors.

Modernize core commercial processes

Companies pursuing this archetype deploy state-of-the-art analytics to optimize commercial functions and achieve sustainable sales growth or margin improvements. Data-driven pricing is among the most common applications in this area.

Take the example of a global distributor with operations in over 30 countries and annual revenues in the magnitude of $10 billion. At first, the company's pricing group made little use of the wealth of data that was available, much of it stored in the cloud. During the transformation, the group created a new end-to-end tech stack, established a center of pricing excellence, and developed a new commercial playbook. The project team identified a total opportunity exceeding $100 million annually. In a pilot, a margin increase of up to 50 percent was observed, while no volume was lost.

In another case, a maker of high-tech hardware implemented a partly automated solution to compare prices and derive recommendations for thousands of product configurations. Key features included configuration-based price benchmarking, price-trend analysis, prescriptive analytics to generate competitive pricing recommendations across B2B2C channels and B2C channels, and automatic weekly updates of up to 200,000 price points for up to 20,000 products. The new, data-driven approach allowed the company to reallocate significant resources from manual pricing management to growth initiatives.

Key success factor: Invest in training and ongoing support once the new approach is rolled out to the front line. This is because data-driven pricing is often met with skepticism or resistance from veteran sales teams, who are used to relying on experience and gut feeling rather than data and analytics.

Redesign the customer journey

Increasingly, B2B customers across industries demand a different kind of service from their suppliers. In a recent McKinsey survey, B2B purchasing officers said that they want less in-person support than many sales teams assume. For simple or repeat purchases of products and services, the vast majority of buyers (85 percent) do not require in-person support.

Many B2B customers now expect the same kind of convenience, speed, flexibility, and transparency they are used to from shopping on popular consumer platforms. More than anything, customers want faster service. According to our survey, "slow response time" is the issue that frustrates them most in their interactions with suppliers (named by 40 percent of all participants, ahead of "pricing issues," named by 19 percent).

For suppliers, this evolution of interaction preferences is an opportunity to transform the customer experience, improve satisfaction, prevent churn, and reduce the cost to serve (Exhibit 4). Take the example of a leading manufacturer of agricultural products with annual revenues in the magnitude of $20 billion. The company was struggling with poor customer satisfaction and an erosion of the customer base. To identify the root causes of dissatisfaction and transform the customer experience, the company set up an agile studio. The cross-functional team comprised customer experts, user-experience designers, supply-chain experts, data scientists, developers, and IT architects.

Exhibit 4

Develop a clear view of what matters to the customer.

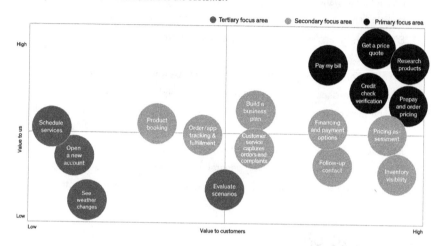

Using agile methodology and design thinking, the team reinvented the customer journey and created a seamless online process for ordering, tracking, and query management. As a result of this effort, the company's customer satisfaction score increased by 24 percentage points, while throughput improved by 20 percent. A minimum-viable-product (MVP)[4] version of the new process went live after 16 weeks.

Key success factors:

1. Use both internal and external data sources to create a 360-degree view of customers, and let unmet needs guide the digitization of the customer journey (customer-back approach):

   o What do customers care about the most?

   o In which areas are they open to digitally enabled process streamlining?

- How can new technology be used to create additional value and pleasant surprises for customers?

2. Use different channels to serve different types of customers, from a portal for registered high-value customers to target offers or flagship e-stores on established B2B portals to reach bargain hunters and generate new leads.

For example, a Fortune 500 industrial-supply company wanted to target small and medium businesses (SMBs), so it set up an online-only business alongside its cross-channel main offering under a new, separate brand. The e-store offers only products that are relevant to SMBs. As a result, the assortment is smaller, simpler, and easier to navigate. The purchasing process itself is hassle free, and orders can be tracked through a mobile app. The company generated significant additional sales to SMBs that had previously shied away from the complexity of the supplier's main offering.

Disrupt the channel

Increasingly, suppliers see digitization as an opportunity to restructure the value chain, especially when it comes to distribution (Exhibit 5). Companies that have previously relied on intermediaries take advantage of digital channels to build direct relations with end customers. That way, they capture additional profit and grow sales.

Exhibit 5

Use digitization to disrupt the channel.

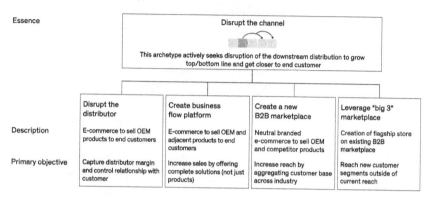

	Disrupt the distributor	Create business flow platform	Create a new B2B marketplace	Leverage "big 3" marketplace
Description	E-commerce to sell OEM products to end customers	E-commerce to sell OEM and adjacent products to end customers	Neutral branded e-commerce to sell OEM and competitor products	Creation of flagship store on existing B2B marketplace
Primary objective	Capture distributor margin and control relationship with customer	Increase sales by offering complete solutions (not just products)	Increase reach by aggregating customer base across industry	Reach new customer segments outside of current reach

One medium-size manufacturer of electrical products was suffering from declining margins because wholesalers and distributors were capturing an increasing share of end-customer revenues. In response, the company created a direct-to-electrician channel and started selling its products directly through an e-commerce channel. The company now controls almost the entire value chain (except for on-site installation), from product design to distribution to licensed electricians. In 2018, the company won six industry awards, including most popular supplier. Electricians rate the supplier 4.9 out of 5 on Trustpilot.

Key success factor: Manage potential conflicts between old and new channels before they arise. Manufacturers should carefully weigh the pros and cons of using an existing B2B platform for distribution. While such platforms bring substantial relevant reach, they can also cannibalize sales that come through other, potentially more profitable channels. If the operator of a platform charges high commission fees or insists on exclusive distribution rights, manufacturers should consider launching their own platform or creating an e-commerce channel for direct distribution to end customers.

Build tomorrow's unicorns

In this archetype, companies use their understanding of the industry to develop new ventures, disrupt their own existing business models, and unlock new revenue streams, typically using a stage-gate financing approach. Of all archetypes, this one is most removed from a company's existing operations. This is also why it can be pursued in parallel with other pathways, provided sufficient resources and funds are available.

To build new ventures that have the potential to grow into unicorns, successful players often adopt a venture capitalist's approach. They prioritize opportunities according to their potential value and develop a venture portfolio. The challenge is to keep new businesses sufficiently close to the parent company for them to benefit from its critical mass, yet separate from the corporate hierarchy, in order to foster the entrepreneurial spirit of a start-up company. (See sidebars, "BP's Launchpad" and "Ping An case study: Digitally enabled growth," for two companies successfully using this approach.)

Key success factors: In our experience, corporate start-ups increase their odds of success when they have the following freedoms:

- *Freedom from financial pressure.* Start-up founders often prioritize market share and scale over profit. Research by the McKinsey Global Institute shows that founder-controlled companies have 60 percent faster revenue growth and 40 percent lower returns on invested capital than widely held companies. But if the parent company pressures its new businesses to deliver short-term return on investment (ROI), founders will be more likely to make decisions that limit long-term growth prospects.

- *Freedom from red tape.* A parent company's bureaucracy can diminish one of the most powerful qualities that typical start-ups possess: the ability to make quick decisions. Every hour that a start-up's employees spend filling out forms or awaiting permission from a corporate functionary is an hour they aren't spending on product development or other value-creating activities.

- *Freedom to source talent.* No corporate start-up should be required to fill its ranks with staff from the parent company. A start-up's hiring decisions should rest with the leadership team. That way, the start-up can draw from pools of workers who are disinclined to seek jobs at traditional companies and unfamiliar to corporate recruiters.

Enablers to deliver impact at scale

In addition to the strategies and skill sets that are specific to the different archetypes, our analysis of top digital performers in B2B has revealed four enablers that help create strategic advantages, de-bottleneck digital transformations, and deliver impact at scale (Exhibit 6):

- *Talent: build bench of technologists and translators.* Successful enterprises excel at attracting and developing best-in-class digital talent, including translators who help bridge the gap between experts and executives. New talent is especially important to overcome organizational inertia and foster innovation that goes beyond the established route to market or beyond the existing business. (For more, read "Analytics translator: The new must-have role.")

- *Agility: use agile teams for technology delivery.* Traditionally, many B2B companies rely on fixed, sequential processes and ways of working. To accelerate digital transformations, companies should take advantage of more flexible, adaptive models in which resources are deployed based on value-creation opportunities, rather than on protocol. (For more, read "Building agile capabilities: The fuel to power your agile 'body'.")

- *Technology: decouple the legacy technology stack.* The most successful players in our sample pursue an approach where the platforms for new digital solutions are decoupled from slower legacy systems. This allows companies to develop MVPs more quickly and add new use cases as opportunities arise. (For more, read "Perpetual evolution—the management approach required for digital transformation.")

- *Data: extend to external, unstructured, proprietary data.* Digital pioneers extend the database beyond the most common sources, such as customer and transaction data. They also leverage product-related data, sales-force performance indicators, communication metadata, and data from external sources, such as social media, market reports, weather forecasts, and competitor offerings. (For more, read "Five fifty: The data disconnect.")

Exhibit 6

Each archetype relies on four enablers to unlock digital growth and impact at scale.

	Archetype	Approach	Critical talent	New ways of working	Data capabilities	Technology needs
A	Modernize core commercial processes	Studio logic	Data engineers Data architects Data engineers	Set up a digital and analytics center of excellence Upgrade commercial playbooks Train workforce through "field-and-forum" approach and Digital and Analytics Academy	Extend sources to external, unstructured, and proprietary data	Start fast with current tech stack and add extraction layer
B	Digitize to differentiate experience	Studio logic	User experience designer Agile coaches Tech-stack architects	Envision digital customer journey through design-thinking approach	Integrate customer interaction and satisfaction data	Upgrade tech stack and add extraction layer for seamless customer interactions
C	Disrupt the channel	Build, operate, transfer	Go-to-market/channel-manage-ment experts Tech-stack architects	Build and operate channels before transfer to business Manage conflicts of new and old channels	Define value proposition based on 360-degree customer-view data Create common marketplace	Integrate tech stack of procurement, supply chain, and commercial
D	Create unicorns	Business-building methodology	Experienced entrepreneurs Business-building specialists	Define venture portfolio Ring-fence venture into business-building incubator	Identify growth opportunities Define data requirements from scratch	Build best-of-breed tech setting based on assembly of standard solutions/tools

Outlook: Do it like you mean it

For manufacturers and providers of services, digitization is at least as much an opportunity as it is a threat. To fortify their position, they should shape the change and think big. They should be prepared to reinvent the way they serve their customers, either by redesigning the customer experience or establishing a direct channel. They should also be willing to go against the grain of existing organizational structures to create the optimal setup for the digitization archetype they choose to pursue.

Traditional company, new businesses: The pairing that can ensure an incumbent's survival

By Philipp Hillenbrand, <u>Dieter Kiewell</u>, Rory Miller-Cheevers, <u>Ivan Ostojic</u>, and Gisa Springer

To guard against disruption, established companies should launch new businesses that have start-up–like freedom—along with access to advantages that start-ups usually lack.

T he list of long-established companies that have been disrupted by fast-moving, tech-enabled powerhouses gets longer by the day. Facing pressure from younger, more innovative challengers, many incumbent companies in the energy sector are also reinventing themselves through a dual effort to digitize their legacy businesses and create new enterprises. Indeed, McKinsey research shows that top-performing companies in various industries divide their capital evenly between transforming their core businesses and developing new ones. Yet few established energy players have managed to turn breakthrough concepts into billion-dollar growth engines that could help secure their long-term survival.

What keeps companies that aren't digital natives from hatching unicorns? Their capacity for innovation isn't necessarily constrained by a lack of good ideas. Many invest huge sums in research. They also seek outsiders' ideas by starting incubators and venture funds and buying start-ups. Rather than a shortage of inspiration, we've observed that older companies' main challenges are an excess of institutional control and an inability to scale up innovations. In a recent McKinsey survey, many respondents said parent companies had hindered the development of their start-ups and limited entrepreneurs' freedom to make decisions.

To overcome the scale-up challenge and respond to the threat of disruption, companies must rethink their operating model for innovation-led growth. The most effective models combine a strategic innovation process with multiple mechanisms for powering innovation development and scale-up. A crucial mechanism we've seen companies establish is an in-house "factory" for building and scaling up disruptive new businesses in ways that corporate accelerators and incubators normally don't.

Such a factory doesn't only assemble the resources and talent to help entrepreneurs start businesses and navigate the early stages of growth. Unlike a conventional accelerator or incubator, the factory also serves as a buffer that shields new enterprises from the unnecessary bureaucratic burdens that can interfere with a start-up's ways of working while endowing these enterprises with the advantages of the parent company's scale (Exhibit 1). In this article, we'll offer our insights on how established companies are using factories to create disruptive businesses with the growth potential to counter the pressures of digital competition.

Exhibit 1

A winning formula for building new businesses combines the methods and pace of successful tech start-ups with the scale of long-standing companies.

The winning formula

Doing things differently ...
- The right opportunities
- The right technology and data architecture
- The right talent

... at a faster pace
- Agile ways of working and organizing
- Customer acquisition
- Full alignment of interests

Unnecessary burdens
- Mind-sets
- Process
- Politics
- IT

The advantages of the parent company's scale
- Customers
- Distribution
- Intellectual property
- Brand
- Negotiating leverage

Success

Ideally, these elements will be provided by a business-building factory that promotes collaboration and gives start-ups the autonomy and freedom to try new approaches

---

A look at BP's business-building unit

BP's upstream digital transformation is well underway, achieved in part through a number of homegrown technologies focused on production optimization. Supported by a multiyear research program, one technology harnesses fiber-optic sensing to listen to sounds deep in the subsurface. By identifying distinct acoustic signatures for sand, fluid, and gas, the technology can precisely locate each substance entering a well so corrective action can be taken.

Early trials in 2014 and 2015 proved the technology's value in several oil fields, bringing wells back online that had been shut down, while increasing production in others. Deployment at scale was elusive, however, with regional businesses seeking additional trials and assurances prior to committing. R&D teams often identify one or two early-adopting business units relatively easily, but building a track record can be more challenging.

In 2018, BP set up a new business-building unit, focusing entirely on scale-up. The acoustic-sensing technology was a prime candidate, given its market potential and intellectual property.

With coaching and support, the original inventors of the technology became cofounders of a new business, scoping the value proposition, securing executive approval, hiring talent, accelerating their tech stack, and using agile to rapidly expand the service offer and deployment model.

The new venture brings the best of both worlds. On the one hand, it benefits from the substantial infrastructure, expertise, and relationships that a large company affords, opening doors to an extensive network of customers. This advantage is then coupled with autonomy, setting aside some of the typical burdens and baggage that might come with this backing. Operating as a stand-alone start-up, the business has scaled fast and is on course to deliver significant value to BP in its first year.

Why long-standing companies are entering the start-up race

The push by BP and other large companies to create disruptive businesses by following the start-up playbook represents a crucial response to the emergence of nimble, inventive enterprises that use powerful technology tools to roil once-stable sectors.   Some of the most dominant winners are the new tech giants, which exploit network effects to make bold forays across industry lines and wrest market share from incumbents.   Moreover, these tech giants continue launching new businesses by staying true to the start-up DNA that made them successful: they empower people to rapidly pursue their commercial ideas without being stifled by the legacy organization.

The disruptive threat from very young companies is nearly as menacing. The average unicorn —a company valued at $1 billion or more in private markets—is just six years old, and the market capitalization of unicorns has increased nearly ninefold in the five years since their IPOs.

The rapid growth of newer companies is also reflected in the turnover of the S&P 500 index. In the late 1970s, the organizations in the S&P 500 index had been on that list for an average of approximately 35 years. Today, the average tenure is closer to 20 years (Exhibit 2). Another telling fact: during the past five years, companies in the S&P Global 1200 that were founded within the past 30 years generated four times as much shareholder value as longer-standing companies.

Exhibit 2

Organic growth has eluded many long-standing companies, and younger companies are outperforming these more established players.

The speed of disruption is accelerating ...

Median age of S&P top 10, 2000	Median age of S&P top 10, 2018	Average S&P 500 tenure by 2027	Average age of a unicorn start-up	5-year valuation growth in post-IPO unicorns[1]
85	**33**	**12**	**6**	**8.7**
years	years	years	years	x

... causing a steady decrease in the tenure of S&P 500-listed companies

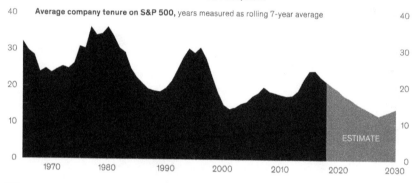

40   Average company tenure on S&P 500, years measured as rolling 7-year average   40

[1]McKinsey research on previous unicorns that have been publicly traded for 5 years or more; compares current market capitalization with valuation in last funding round. Source: 3Q 2018 VC Valuations Report, PitchBook Data, November 14, 2018, pitchbook.com; Innosight Holdings; McKinsey analysis

Amid this boom, large companies have stepped up their attempts to tap the value-creating prowess of entrepreneurs. (This approach isn't new. In the late 1990s, for example, big businesses rushed to create start-up incubators, acquire fast-growing internet companies, and set up venture-investing units.) To take one measure of their activity, the number of corporate venture-capital (CVC) organizations making their first investments increased from 64 in 2013 to 264 in 2018.   In a recent McKinsey survey of executives involved with CVCs, incubators, and accelerators, 92 percent of respondents agreed that their companies had seen a significant increase in the financial value of the enterprises in which they had invested.

However, the survey also found that corporate business-building activities are often hampered by certain challenges associated with working in a legacy organization. Almost half of the respondents said internal policies had slowed the development of new businesses. Less than 10 percent said their companies had given start-ups full freedom to operate.

Nor are established companies consistently giving their start-ups the kind of support that could help them gain an edge. One-quarter of respondents said the parent company had not enabled its start-ups to capture even one advantage from the parent company's scale, compared with the support they might have received from private investors. Just 25 percent strongly agreed that their companies had the capabilities to deliver advantages associated with scale. Respondents most often cited a mismatch of expectations or ways of working as the reason why parent companies and start-ups had found it difficult to collaborate effectively (Exhibit 3).

Exhibit 3

Executives report that traditional companies seldom make it easy for in-house start-ups to operate and capitalize on the parent company's advantages.

Building new businesses is a high priority of senior management

But the large-company setting is not always favorable: internal policies tend to slow growth, and new businesses are not granted autonomy to act

| have been engaged in business building for 5+ years | agree that new-venture building has brought significant financial value | agree that their businesses are subject to the same policies (eg, HR), with almost half of all respondents claiming politics slow down the process of growth | agree that businesses must get input from stakeholders across the corporate group to execute day-to-day decisions |

Against this backdrop, many companies are struggling to convert their strengths into advantages for their new businesses

"We are a large multinational, and as such, we are subject to the traditional silos and focus on individual lines of business success, sometimes at the expense of the new-venture-growth opportunities"

"We face struggles with core-company approach vs new-venture need to operate differently"

"Influencing the strategic decision-making process while maintaining the venture's flexibility of operations at the same time becomes a challenging task, especially during incubation"

Source: McKinsey survey of 93 C-level and vice president/executive vice president–level executives (representing more than 70 companies) with direct control over business-building activities at their organizations.

New enterprises and traditional companies: Understanding the mismatch

As previously noted, start-ups innovate and scale rapidly by adhering to priorities and methods that don't fit neatly in traditional companies. But if executives can better understand the new breed of start-ups, they can adjust their business-building approaches to suit these enterprises.

Today's new-business template

The young companies that have grown the fastest in recent years typically exhibit six defining features.

A compelling business opportunity. Our experience suggests that fast-growing start-ups target opportunities that lie at the nexus of three considerations: a large market that can be unlocked in incremental steps, a technology model that takes advantage of ecosystems, and a clear path toward attractive monetization.

A modern technology stack. One advantage that start-ups enjoy over established companies is that they build their technology stacks from scratch, rather than having to work with legacy IT. Our experience suggests that it is possible to assemble modular, off-the-shelf components and some proprietary code into a high-performance technology stack capable of supporting the initial minimum-viable-product stage in just three or four weeks.

Adaptable talent. The strongest start-ups we've seen are led by people who are comfortable managing uncertainty by following test-and-learn methods and who are willing to accept failures made for the sake of learning. They are also able to hire and motivate diverse specialists (designers, product owners, software developers, data scientists, salespeople, and so on). These qualities matter more than a particular industry background—not least because founders mustn't hesitate to reorient their enterprises when they find better opportunities beyond the industry where they first intended to compete. In a McKinsey interview, Aaron Levie, CEO of the cloud-storage company Box, said, "In the first year and a half of the company, I would say every 48 hours we'd change our business model."

Fast-paced operations. Speed of learning is a vital factor in a start-up's success because first movers and fast followers gain major advantages amid digital competition. In a McKinsey interview, José Filippini, the CFO of Youse, a direct-to-consumer insurtech business launched by Brazilian financial leader Caixa Seguradora, said, "We also based the decision to launch Youse on the clear idea that there is strategic advantage in being the first mover." (For more on Youse, see sidebar "Youse: Digital innovation in Brazil's insurance market.")

Since new businesses typically operate in uncharted commercial spaces, they must follow truly agile methods (as opposed to methods that many companies label agile but include only some facets of agile) to refine their products over many test-and-learn cycles. As Box CEO

Aaron Levie told McKinsey, "There was a lot of early constant iterating, constant pivoting of the business. That became one of our core values as a company."

An agile customer-acquisition funnel. New businesses scale up rapidly by using agile methods and low-cost digital channels to attract and retain customers. The ability to rapidly iterate offerings and quickly acquire large numbers of customers is integral to winning market share from slower-moving incumbents.

Alignment of interests. The rapid change that people experience at start-ups can be thrilling as well as draining. Start-ups foster resilience in their people partly by offering them incentives—notably, equity stakes—to persevere. "[The] thing that actually unlocks human potential is when people feel they have control over their own destiny and they can make a killing if they really succeed on their wild bet," says Bill Gross, founder of Idealab.

Unnecessary burdens and overlooked advantages: Why corporate start-ups often come up short

Even when new enterprises follow the described template, we have seen them struggle inside traditional companies for two main reasons.

The first reason is that traditional companies make it difficult for new businesses to follow the very practices that might make them successful. Scott Cook, the cofounder and executive-committee chairman of Intuit, described this phenomenon in a McKinsey interview: "Normally, companies put up a phalanx of barriers and hurdles and mountains to climb that may not seem hard for the boss or the CEO but are intensely hard, impossibly hard, for our young innovator to conquer."   Imagine an in-house start-up that draws up a cloud-based technology stack—but can't build it, because the parent company's chief information officer insists that the start-up operate in the enterprise-IT environment.

Sometimes naysayers at the parent company undermine start-ups. Sam Yagan, former CEO of Match, witnessed this dynamic after Match founded Tinder, a mobile dating app. In an interview with McKinsey, he said, "When we launched Tinder inside of Match, we found that there was resistance from some people inside the core business who saw Tinder as a threat—maybe to the business, maybe to their own expertise in the company, and certainly to the culture."

Some parent companies do treat their start-ups as nearly independent entities, which helps them avoid unnecessary burdens. Unfortunately, this arm's-length relationship can also prevent start-ups from capitalizing on the advantages they can gain from the parent company's scale, such as a customer base and brand recognition (more on these follows).

The inability to seize these advantages is the second reason why we often see corporate start-ups underperform.

A factory for building and scaling up new businesses

Although many corporate start-ups are too young to have reached massive scale by now, we have seen long-standing companies support the scaling of new businesses by establishing a dedicated business-building factory. The factory nurtures a portfolio of businesses by evaluating proposals, choosing which ones to back, working with the founders to develop business cases, securing funding from the parent company, hiring an initial team, and coaching founders.

While these activities resemble those of a corporate accelerator or incubator, the business-building factory is positioned and staffed differently. A typical accelerator or incubator sits in a business unit and is led by a manager three or four tiers below the C-suite, with little or no authority to drive pace and unlock the advantages of scale. By contrast, a business-building factory should be positioned as a relatively independent, empowered arm of the company, staffed with several types of personnel:

- *Experienced entrepreneurs hired from outside the parent company.* Their main responsibilities are to help evaluate and prioritize business ideas and hire founders. They also coach founders through the typical ups and downs of scaling a new venture.

- *Influential, well-connected executives from the parent company.* In addition to representing the company as the controlling shareholder of each new business, these executives serve as advocates for the start-ups within the parent company. That role involves contacting other executives when a start-up must work around a bureaucratic requirement or tap the parent company's advantages and making sure that those executives understand the start-up's needs and that they accommodate them.

- *Specialists in business-building disciplines, such as design thinking, product ownership, software development, system and data architecture, data science, sales, and marketing.* These specialists make up a pool of shared staff who assist each start-up until it grows large enough to hire specialists of its own.

The position and staffing of the factory ensure that the new businesses are unburdened by the corporate bureaucracy and endowed with the parent company's advantages. The next sections offer a closer look at these two duties.

Liberating new businesses from the unnecessary burdens of bureaucracy

In our experience, corporate start-ups increase their odds of success when they have few, if any, obligations to the legacy features of the parent company. Ideally, the factory will give new businesses the autonomy of independent start-ups. At minimum, the executives in the factory will use their clout to ensure that new businesses have three types of freedom from the parent company.

Freedom from financial pressure. Start-up founders often prioritize market share and scale over profits. Research by the McKinsey Global Institute shows that among NASDAQ-listed software and internet companies, founder-controlled companies have 60 percent faster revenue growth and 35 to 40 percent lower profit margins and returns on invested capital than widely held companies.   But if the parent company pressures its new businesses to deliver short-term returns on investment, founders will be more likely to make decisions that limit a new business's long-term prospects.

Freedom from red tape. A parent company's bureaucracy can diminish one of the most powerful qualities that typical start-ups possess: the ability to make quick decisions. Every hour that a start-up's employees spend filling out forms or awaiting permission from a corporate functionary is an hour they aren't spending on product development or other value-creating activities. Parent companies should therefore refrain from imposing their requirements on new businesses (except for requirements related to legal and regulatory mandates).

Freedom to source talent. No corporate start-up should be required to fill its ranks with staff from the parent company. A start-up's hiring decisions should rest with the leadership team. That way, the start-up can draw from pools of workers who are disinclined to seek jobs at traditional companies and unfamiliar to corporate recruiters.

Unlocking the parent company's advantages

Established companies can bestow on their new businesses advantages that independent start-ups can't easily replicate. While the advantages that a start-up might need will vary, five generally stand out as especially valuable.

Customer relationships. A corporate start-up can gain an advantage with customers if the parent company positions the start-up's offerings as a complement to its own. For example, Royal FloraHolland, a large flower-growing and trading cooperative, had observed that growers and buyers were finding it more complicated to conduct direct trades because the network of trading platforms was becoming more fragmented. In response, the cooperative built a unified digital marketplace for auctions and direct trading of horticultural products. The new marketplace scaled up quickly because it brought growers and buyers onto a single platform and integrated with Royal FloraHolland's existing services. "By enabling our customers to thrive in the digital economy, we're reinventing our business for the future," said Gerhard van der Bijl, chief digital officer of Royal FloraHolland. (For more on Royal FloraHolland's digital marketplace, see sidebar "Floriday: A digital hub for horticultural trade.")

Distribution capabilities. If a corporate start-up's offerings complement the parent company's or can be distributed in a similar manner, then the new business can piggyback on the parent company's distribution system.

Intellectual property. Established companies possess intellectual capital—including data, technical know-how, and patents—that can benefit start-ups. Knowledge sharing between a parent company and a new venture worked well for ABN AMRO Bank, a large European bank, when it set up a digital-lending subsidiary called New10. New10 kept most of its operations separate from those of ABN AMRO Bank: it recruited and onboarded its own people, formed its own vendor relationships, and set up an entirely new technology architecture. But when it came time to establish other core capabilities, such as regulatory compliance and fraud management, New10 relied on the expertise of ABN AMRO Bank's compliance and risk functions. "Bringing in ABN AMRO Bank's expertise enabled New10 to develop our proposition more quickly than a stand-alone company could have and to offer attractive pricing and experiences to customers on the day we launched," said Patrick Pfaff, New10's founder. (For more on New10, see sidebar "New10: A digital-lending start-up in the Netherlands.")

Brand strength. An established company's brand can confer legitimacy on a start-up that helps it win customers. New10's marketing team also linked the new lending institution with ABN AMRO Bank, which helped New10 earn recognition as the "most desired brand" for lending to small and medium-size enterprises in the Netherlands.

Negotiating leverage. Start-ups can't match the purchasing power of large companies—or the scale they can offer potential partners.

The more a start-up relies on its parent company for assistance, the more difficult it can become for the start-up to maintain autonomy. A start-up that wishes to market to the parent company's customers, for example, might need permission from uncooperative account managers. Executive members of the factory can urge fellow executives to have their functions or business units provide start-ups with the assistance they need.

Another helpful practice is for the factory to enlist representatives of parent-company functions as liaisons to the new businesses, with responsibility for ascertaining their needs and coordinating functional support. The liaison's job should be a formal part-time role, or even a full-time role (if the parent company has a large portfolio of new businesses), with goals and incentives linked to the factory's performance.

"[Big] companies will never do something substantial or worth thinking about or worth writing a history book about in their core businesses," said venture capitalist Steve Jurvetson in a McKinsey interview. "But the beauty is that it doesn't mean big companies are dead; it just means big companies need to innovate outside their core businesses."   Innovating outside the core, however, is easier said than done. Too often, the legacy organization throttles business-building efforts and shuts would-be entrepreneurs out of departments that could give their start-ups an edge. To better the odds that new businesses will strengthen a parent company's financial prospects and strategic positioning, traditional companies can house their enterprises inside a factory that shelters them from bureaucratic burdens and provides them with the advantages of the parent organization's scale and know-how. Such a factory can provide long-standing companies with a renewable source of fast-growing business models that will sustain them in the turbulence of digital disruption.

Refrences

- Interviews with 60 C-suite executives and quantitative surveys with another 200, February–May 2019.
- McKinsey analysis based on 2017 Spencer Stuart U.S. Board Index, 2018 PwC's publication, "Board composition: Consider the value of younger directors on your board," and Kimberly A. Whitler, Ryan Krause, & Donald R. Lehmann's article, "When and How Board Members with Marketing Experience Facilitate Firm Growth."
- Scott Keller and Mary Meaney, " Attracting and retaining the right talent ," The McKinsey Quarterly, November 2017.

- McKinsey analysis.
- Marc Goedhart and Tim Koller, " The value premium of organic growth ," McKinsey & Company, January 2017.
- The Growth Opportunity Scanner is a proprietary McKinsey solution that maps market, category, and competitors and identifies opportunities for growth.

- Patrick Viguerie, Sven Smit, and Mehrdad Baghai, The Granularity of Growth, Marshall Cavendish/Cyan, 2007.
- Brian Gregg, Hussein Kalaoui, Joel Maynes, and Gustavo Schuler, " Marketing's Holy Grail: Digital personalization at scale ," McKinsey & Company, November 2016.
- Kabir Ahuja, Jesko Perrey, and Liz Hilton Segel, " Invest, Create, Perform: Mastering the three dimensions of growth in the digital age , " McKinsey & Company, March 2017.7. Kabir Ahuja, Biljana Cvetanovski, Jesko Perrey, and Liz Hilton Segel, " Building an engine for growth that funds itself ," McKinsey & Company, May 2018.
- Yuval Atsmon, " How nimble resource allocation can double your company's value , " McKinsey & Company, August 2016.
- Biljana Cvetanovski, Stacey Haas, Max Magni, and Cathy Wu, " Marketing's hidden treasure: Better CPE can unlock millions to fuel growth ," McKinsey & Company, June 2018.
- Gerald Chappell, Holger Harreis, András Havas, Andrea Nuzzo, Theo Pepanides, and Kayvaun Rowshankish. " The lending revolution: How digital credit is changing banks from the inside ," McKinsey & Company, August 2018.

- Gadi Benmark, Sebastian Klapdor, Mathias Kullmann, and Ramji Sundararajan, " How retailers can drive profitable growth through dynamic pricing ," McKinsey & Company, March 2017.
- Christopher Angevine, Candace Lun Plotkin, and Jennifer Stanley, " The secret to making it in the digital sales world: The human touch ," in Driving above-market growth in B2B, McKinsey & Company, May 2018.
- " Growing beyond the core business ," McKinsey & Company, July 2015.
- Benedict Sheppard, Hugo Sarrazin, Garen Kouyoumjian, and Fabricio Dore, " The business value of design ," McKinsey & Company, October 2018.
- Mark Dziersk, Stacey Haas, Jon McClain, and Brian Quinn, " From lab to leader: How consumer companies can drive growth at scale with disruptive innovation ," McKinsey & Company, September 2018.
- Kabir Ahuja, Jesko Perrey, and Liz Hilton Segel, " Invest, create, perform: Mastering the three dimensions of growth in the digital age , " McKinsey & Company, March 2017.
- Jacques Bughin, Eric Hazan, Susan Lund, Peter Dahlström, Anna Weisinger, and Amresh Subramaniam, Skill Shift: Automation and the future of the workforce, McKinsey Global Institute, May 2018.
- Benedict Sheppard, Hugo Sarrazin, Garen Kouyoumjian, and Fabricio Dore, " The business value of design ," McKinsey & Company, October 2018.
- Benedict Sheppard, John Edson, and Garen Kouyoumjian, " More than a feeling: Ten design practices to deliver business value ," McKinsey & Company, December 2017.
- McKinsey analysis on Nielsen xAOC data, 20142017, US CPG manufacturers— food, beverage, personal care, and household care.
- McKinsey analysis on Nielsen xAOC data, 20142017, US CPG manufacturers— food, beverage, personal care, and household care.
- McKinsey analysis on Nielsen xAOC data, 20142017, US CPG manufacturers— food, beverage, personal care, and household care.
- Survey, " Growing beyond the core business ," July 2015, McKinsey.com.
- The online survey was in the field from March 616, 2018, and garnered responses from 1,937 participants working at private-sector companies and representing the full range of regions, company sizes, functional specialties, and tenures. Of them, 1,466 work in industries where our questions on organic growth were most relevant to their businesses and reported their companies' rate of organic revenue growth compared with the overall sector's, so their responses were included in our main analysis. Those surveyed whose responses were not included in our main analysis work in professional services, the public sector, and the social sector. To

adjust for differences in response rates, the data are weighted by the contribution of each respondent's nation to global GDP.

- Kabir Ahuja, Jesko Perrey, and Liz Hilton Segel, " Invest, Create, Perform: Mastering the three dimensions of growth in the digital age , " March 2017, McKinsey.com.
- A company's primary lens is the one for which respondents reported the highest number of effective or very effective best practices. For the Invest lens, we asked about seven best practices; for Perform, eight; and for Create, six.
- We define "mastery" as respondents' agreement that 70 percent or more of the best practices in a given lens describe their companies.
- For more on mastery of the three lenses, see Abhinav Goel, Duncan Miller, and Ryan Paulowsky," Choosing the right path to growth , " McKinsey Quarterly, October 2018, McKinsey.com.
- Based on " Reborn in the cloud ," McKinsey interview, July 2015, McKinsey.com
- .8. Mehrdad Baghai, Sven Smit, and S. Patrick Viguerie, " The granularity of growth ," book excerpt, McKinsey Quarterly, March 2008, McKinsey.com.
- Respondents working in below-average sectors report a 43.8 percent adoption rate for the capabilities the survey asked about. Among the above-average sectors, respondents report an average adoption rate of 48.1 percent of capabilities.
- McKinsey analysis.
- Marc Goedhart and Tim Koller, " The value premium of organic growth ," McKinsey & Company, January 2017.
- The Growth Opportunity Scanner is a proprietary McKinsey solution that maps market, category, and competitors and identifies opportunities for growth.
- Patrick Viguerie, Sven Smit, and Mehrdad Baghai, The Granularity of Growth, Marshall Cavendish/Cyan, 2007.
- Brian Gregg, Hussein Kalaoui, Joel Maynes, and Gustavo Schuler, " Marketing's Holy Grail: Digital personalization at scale ," McKinsey & Company, November 2016.
- Kabir Ahuja, Jesko Perrey, and Liz Hilton Segel, " Invest, Create, Perform: Mastering the three dimensions of growth in the digital age , " McKinsey & Company, March 2017.
- Kabir Ahuja, Biljana Cvetanovski, Jesko Perrey, and Liz Hilton Segel, " Building an engine for growth that funds itself ," McKinsey & Company, May 2018.
- Yuval Atsmon, " How nimble resource allocation can double your company's value , " McKinsey & Company, August 2016.
- Biljana Cvetanovski, Stacey Haas, Max Magni, and Cathy Wu, " Marketing's hidden treasure: Better CPE can unlock millions to fuel growth ," McKinsey & Company, June 2018.

- Gerald Chappell, Holger Harreis, András Havas, Andrea Nuzzo, Theo Pepanides, and Kayvaun Rowshankish. " The lending revolution: How digital credit is changing banks from the inside ," McKinsey & Company, August 2018.
- Gadi Benmark, Sebastian Klapdor, Mathias Kullmann, and Ramji Sundararajan, " How retailers can drive profitable growth through dynamic pricing ," McKinsey & Company, March 2017.
- Christopher Angevine, Candace Lun Plotkin, and Jennifer Stanley, " The secret to making it in the digital sales world: The human touch ," in Driving above-market growth in B2B, McKinsey & Company, May 2018.
- " Growing beyond the core business ," McKinsey & Company, July 2015.
- Benedict Sheppard, Hugo Sarrazin, Garen Kouyoumjian, and Fabricio Dore, " The business value of design ," McKinsey & Company, October 2018.
- Mark Dziersk, Stacey Haas, Jon McClain, and Brian Quinn, " From lab to leader: How consumer companies can drive growth at scale with disruptive innovation ," McKinsey & Company, September 2018.
- Kabir Ahuja, Jesko Perrey, and Liz Hilton Segel, " Invest, create, perform: Mastering the three dimensions of growth in the digital age , " McKinsey & Company, March 2017.
- Jacques Bughin, Eric Hazan, Susan Lund, Peter Dahlström, Anna Weisinger, and Amresh Subramaniam, Skill Shift: Automation and the future of the workforce, McKinsey Global Institute, May 2018.
- Benedict Sheppard, Hugo Sarrazin, Garen Kouyoumjian, and Fabricio Dore, " The business value of design ," McKinsey & Company, October 2018.
- Benedict Sheppard, John Edson, and Garen Kouyoumjian, " More than a feeling: Ten design practices to deliver business value ," McKinsey & Company, December 2017.
- See Dominic Dodd and Ken Favaro, The Three Tensions: Winning the Struggle to Perform Without Compromise, first edition, San Francisco, CA: Jossey-Bass, 2007.
- Agency problems emerge when an agent is required to make decisions for another person or group, whose information, preferences, and interests may not be aligned with the agent's.
- We measure profit as NOPLAT—net operating profit less adjusted taxes. Invested capital comprises operating invested capital of $6,660 million and goodwill and intangibles of $2,602 million. In other words, 28 percent of the capital of a typical company represents additional value over book value paid in acquisitions.
- We asked companies to determine their growth strategy, providing the option of choosing more than one. We then asked respondents to indicate how much each strategy contributed to their growth in percentage terms.

- We asked companies to determine their growth strategy, providing the option of choosing more than one. We then asked respondents to indicate how much each strategy contributed to their growth in percentage terms.
- We grouped 550 large US and European companies into thirds based on total revenue growth. We then ranked the companies in each tercile by their increase in goodwill and intangibles as a proxy for acquired growth, and again broke them into thirds based on their level of acquired growth. We then compared the median TRS for each of the nine groups. Since our proxy is imprecise, the chart shows the TRS only for those companies with the most and least organic and acquired growth. The sample excludesthe banking and insurance sectors, which severely underperformed in this period because of the 2008 financial crisis. It also excludes the extraction and commodity sectors because their performance is strongly affected by commodity price cycles.
- There is a selection bias in our sample: not all companies that invest in organic growth actually realize that growth.
- In related research, McKinsey looked at the share-price performance of 500 US and European companies over 15 years, which showed that for all levels of revenue growth, those with more organic growth generated higher shareholder returns than those whose growth relied more heavily on acquisitions. For more, see Marc Goedhart and Tim Koller, " The value premium of organic growth ," January 2017.
- We studied dozens of corporate-growth programs and paired those findings with insights from a panel of approximately 1,500 managers and executives globally, across 17 industries. We surveyed executives on 36 practices and capabilities that supported their growth strategies. About half were foundational capabilities such as contract management and transactional pricing. The rest were advanced capabilities that supported the three key levers or approaches: creativity (6), investment (7), and performance (8). We defined mastery of an individual lever as successful adoption of 70 percent of the supporting practices.
- Top-quartile (exceptional) growth beats industry growth rates by more than four percentage points.
- Fewer than 15 percent of executives in our survey said they were in the top quartile for mastery of all three levers.
- We asked companies to determine their growth strategy, providing the option of choosing more than one. We then asked respondents to indicate how much each strategy contributed to their growth in percentage terms.
- See Ilan Guedj, Jennifer Huang, and Johan Sulaeman, "Internal capital allocation and firm performance," working paper for the International Symposium on Risk Management and Derivatives, October 2009 (revised in March 2010).2. We used

Compustat data on 1,616 US-listed companies with operations in a minimum of two distinct four-digit Standard Industrial Classification (SIC) codes. Resource allocation is measured as 1 minus the minimum percentage of capital expenditure received by distinct business units over the 15-year period. This measure captures the relative amount of capital that can flow across a business over time; the rest of the money is "stuck." Similar results were found with more sophisticated measures that control for sales and asset growth.3. See Dan Lovallo and Olivier Sibony, " The case for behavioral strategy , " March 2010.

- For more, see James Manyika, " Google's CFO on growth, capital structure, and leadership , " August 2011.
- See Claire Cain Miller, "In a quest for focus, Google purges small projects," nytimes.com, November 10, 2011.
- See three publications by Mehrdad Baghai, Sven Smit, and S. Patrick Viguerie: "The granularity of growth," May 2007; The Granularity of Growth: How to Identify the Sources of Growth and Drive Enduring Company Performance, Hoboken, NJ: Wiley, 2008; and " Is your growth strategy flying blind? ," Harvard Business Review, May 2009, Volume 87, Number 5, pp. 8697.
- Chris Bradley , Martin Hirt , and Sven Smit , " Strategy to beat the odds ," McKinsey & Company, February, 2018.
- Jiri Franta, David González, Jesús Rodríguez González, and Rui de Sousa, " Harnessing the power of advanced analytics in electricity networks' asset management ," McKinsey & Company, April 2018.
- Shital Chheda, Ewan Duncan, and Stefan Roggenhofer, " Putting customer experience at the heart of next-generation operating models ," McKinsey & Company, March 2017.
- Federico Berruti, Graeme Nixon, Giambattista Taglioni, and Rob Whiteman, " Intelligent process automation: The engine at the core of the next-generation operating model ," McKinsey & Company, 2017.
- Alexander Edlich, Heiko Heimes, and Allison Watson, " Can you achieve and sustain G&A cost reductions? " McKinsey Quarterly, October 2016.
- Chris Bradley, Martin Hirt, and Sven Smit, " Strategy to beat the odds ,
- For more on how service channels can support revenue growth, see "Elevating customer satisfaction and growth through service to solutions".
- 2019 McKinsey EMEA Data Summit in Barcelona.
- A unicorn is defined as a privately held start-up company valued at $1 billion or more. The term was coined in 2013 by venture capitalist Aileen Lee. The mythical creature is an allusion to the rarity of such successful ventures. In this article, we use the term to refer to new ventures that have the potential to become unicorns.

- See also Jorchen Boringer and Dr. Tjark Freundt, "Kundenführung 4.0: Von Menschen und Maschinen,"perspectives Magazin, January 18, 2018, perspectives.infraserv.com.
- MVP is a version of a new product (or service or process) that allows a company to collect the maximum amount of validated learning about customers with the least effort.
- "BP Launchpad," bp.com.
- Jordan Blum, "BP gets into the startup biz with its new Lytt company," Houston Chronicle, May 8, 2019, houstonchronicle.com.
- "BP recently created BP Launchpad as a business incubator," AZERNEWS, May 10, 2019, azernews.az.
- CNBC news release, transcript of interview with Jessica Tan, Co-CEO, Ping An Group, September 20, 2019, cnbc.com.
- Ping An annual reports and investor resources; McKinsey research.
- The survey asked respondents to indicate how much digital capital their companies had allocated to digitizing core businesses and developing new digital businesses. It identified top-performing companies as those in the top decile for organic revenue growth: 25 percent or more in the past three years. For more, see " A winning operating model for digital strategy ," January 2019.
- Jacques Bughin, Laura LaBerge, and Anette Mellbye, " The case for digital reinvention ," McKinsey Quarterly, February 2017.
- For more, see Venkat Atluri, Miklós Dietz, and Nicolaus Henke, " Competing in a world of sectors without borders ," McKinsey Quarterly, July 2017; and Tushar Bhatia, Mohsin Imtiaz, Eric Kutcher, and Dilip Wagle, " How tech giants deliver outsized returns—and what it means for the rest of us , " September 2017.
- The 2018 Global CVC Report, CB Information Services, February 2019, cbinsights.com.
- The survey was in the field in May and June 2019 and garnered responses from 93 C-suite and vice president/executive vice president–level executives and managers based in France, Germany, Italy, the United Kingdom, and the United States, representing more than 70 companies across a wide range of industries and company sizes. All respondents indicated that they control one or more of their companies' business-building activities (investing in start-ups directly or through corporate venture funds, operating a dedicated incubator that helps internal ideas or pilots become stand-alone ventures, operating a dedicated accelerator that helps younger or smaller ventures to scale up, or otherwise building or creating new ventures).
- " From start-up to scale: A conversation with Box CEO Aaron Levie ," October 2018.

- For more, see Jacques Bughin, Tanguy Catlin, Martin Hirt, and Paul Willmott, " Why digital strategies fail ," McKinsey Quarterly, January 2018.
- Wouter Aghina, Karin Ahlback, Aaron De Smet, Gerald Lackey, Michael Lurie, Monica Murarka, and Christopher Handscomb, The five trademarks of agile organizations , January 2018.
- " From start-up to scale: A conversation with Box CEO Aaron Levie ," October 2018.
- " How big companies can innovate ," February 2015.
- " How big companies can innovate ," February 2015.
- " Building data-driven culture: An interview with ShopRunner CEO Sam Yagan , " McKinsey Quarterly, February 2019.
- For more, see " The new global competition for corporate profits ," McKinsey Global Institute, September 2015.
- " Inside the mind of a venture capitalist ," McKinsey Global Institute, August 2016.
- The Global Implementation Survey included 1,400+ executives, including 500+ C-level executives from 90 countries and 600+ from companies with revenues of > US $1 billion.
- According to an analysis by McKinsey Growth Magnifier team, only 27 percent of companies rely on creation of new products alone, whereas the rest combine new-product creation with superior execution.
- This Commercial Capabilities Assessment Tool , one of the sales solutions built on the Periscope by McKinsey platform, assesses more than 200 marketing and sales practices against industry and global benchmarks.